Lorraine Farrelly

representational
techniques

adj. relating to or characterised
by representation

n. a way of carrying out
a particular task, especially the
execution of an artistic work
or a scientific procedure

An AVA Book

Published by AVA Publishing SA
Rue des Fontenailles 16
Case Postale
1000 Lausanne 6
Switzerland
Telephone: +41 786 005 109
Email: enquiries@avabooks.ch

Distributed by Thames & Hudson
(ex-North America)
181a High Holborn
London WC1V 7QX
United Kingdom
Telephone: +44 20 7845 5000
Fax: +44 20 7845 5055
Email: sales@thameshudson.co.uk
www.thamesandhudson.com

Distributed in the USA & Canada by:
Watson-Guptill Publications
770 Broadway
New York, New York 10003
USA
Fax: +1 646 654 5487
Email: info@watsonguptill.com
www.watsonguptill.com

English Language Support Office
AVA Publishing (UK) Ltd.
Telephone: +44 1903 204 455
Email: enquiries@avabooks.co.uk

ISBN 2-940373-62-0 and
978-2-940373-62-8

10 9 8 7 6 5 4 3 2 1

Design by Jane Harper

Production by AVA Book Production
Pte. Ltd., Singapore
Telephone: +65 6334 8173
Fax: +65 6259 9830
Email: production@avabooks.com.sg

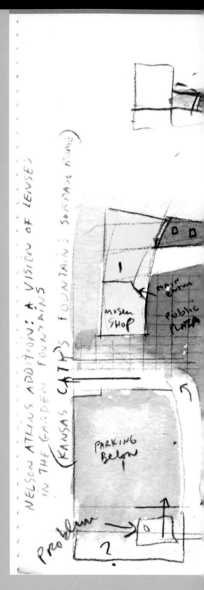

Project: Nelson-Atkins Museum of Art
Location: Kansas City, USA
Architect: Steven Holl Architects
Date: 2007

This image brings together all
aspects of the architectural scheme.
It communicates both the concept
of light used in the museum's interior
galleries and the sense of the
building in the context of its
surrounding landscape.

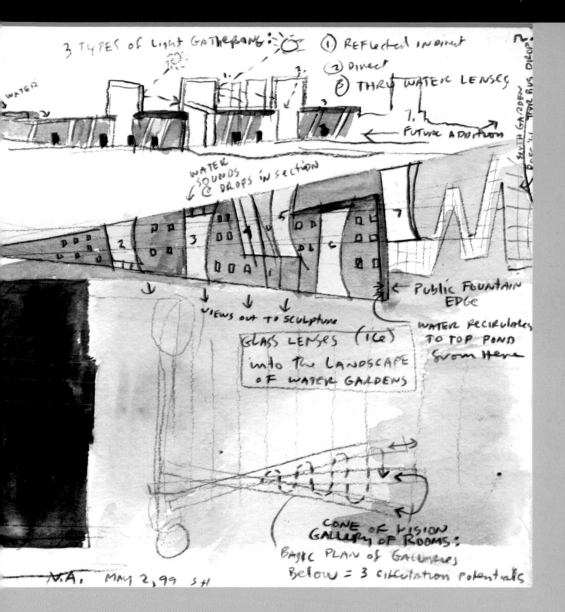

3 TYPES of Light GATHERING: ○ ① REFLECTED INDIRECT

② DIRECT

③ THRU WATER LENSES

WATER

1.

2.

3.

7. ← FUTURE ADDITION

SIXTH GARDEN DOES N' TYPE PLUS DROP

WATER SOUNDS @ DROPS IN SECTION

2 3 5 6 7

A

↓ ↓ ↓ ↓ ↓ ↓ ↓

VIEWS OUT TO SCULPTURE

GLASS LENSES (ICE) into THE LANDSCAPE OF WATER GARDENS

→ ← PUBLIC FOUNTAIN EDGE

WATER RECIRCULATES TO TOP POND FROM HERE

CONE OF VISION
GALLERY OF ROOMS:
BASIC PLAN OF GALLERIES
Below = 3 CIRCULATION POTENTIALS

N.A. MAY 2, 99 SH

Contents

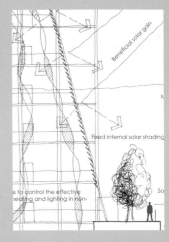

Representational techniques

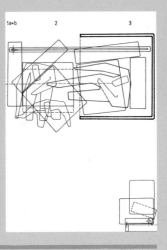

Representation is an important aspect of any visual or design-based discipline and the techniques for representing architectural ideas are both exciting and challenging. Architectural ideas can eventually become buildings. An idea leads to a concept, which becomes a sketch. The sketch is then developed into a physical sketch model and a set of scale drawings that are explored and investigated in detail.

Representing each of these stages of architectural development requires a variety of skills. Sometimes freehand, loose or intuitive drawings and models, where concept and abstraction are critical, are the best techniques to employ. At other times, the precise detail of CAD drawings might be needed to explain how a building is assembled. The challenge of architectural representation is to generate the right type of image to suit the given stage in the design process.

Architectural drawings employ a kind of language, and the right dialect is needed for a given situation. The language of architectural drawing is varied, but the vocabulary is basic. Ideas are expressed as lines and all lines or strokes on a page are careful and considered. The excitement with architectural representation is to use the language of drawing, to perfect it and develop it so it communicates the architectural idea to become a unique, real architectural experience.

As with all drawing techniques, it is important to practise and develop your own skills and adapt methods to different situations. Within each of the book's six sections you will find an exercise, which will allow you to test and apply the ideas; introduced. A sketchbook (ideally one that has blank, thick paper and is A4-size or larger) and pencil are important tools to have to hand. Whenever you draw or make a mark in your sketchbook, keep it, don't erase it. There are no such things as mistakes in drawing. It's all a visual record of your ideas; some will be better than others, but they all contribute towards something bigger and better. If nothing else, you can always look back at the first pages you started in your sketchbook and see how far you have travelled.

Sketch
This section explores ideas of how to sketch and draw at all stages of the design process.

Scale
This section looks at the range of specific drawing scales that can be used at various stages of the architectural design process. Understanding the application of these scales for different situations is critical.

Orthographic projection
Orthographic projection looks at the measured drawings that explain the idea of the building in two-dimensional form: plans, sections and elevations. These two-dimensional drawings reveal the three-dimensional intention of the building.

Three-dimensional images
These are the most easily accessible images and provide a perspective view of a space, which will give an impression of the experience of the building on a particular site or location. Three-dimensional images are also useful for creating construction and assembly drawings.

Modelling
Modelling ideas allow an exploration spatially of concepts, spaces and form at all stages of the design process. Models can be created physically or using CAD software.

Layout and presentation
The communication of the idea is critical. How it is organised and presented is an important design consideration.

Introduction

How to get the most out of this book

This book introduces different aspects of representational techniques in architecture via dedicated chapters for each topic. Each chapter provides examples of the creative use of different representational techniques in architecture at each stage of the design process. The examples shown are contributions from a range of contemporary architects and, together with detailed analysis in the text, form a book that offers a unique insight into the practical and professional world of architectural design.

Chapter openers
These introduce and outline the key information in each chapter.

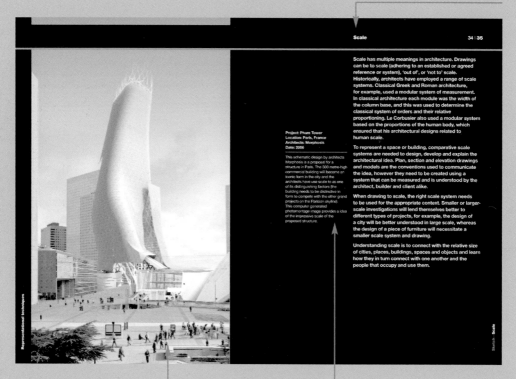

Scale has multiple meanings in architecture. Drawings can be to scale (adhering to an established or agreed reference or system), 'out of', or 'not to' scale. Historically, architects have employed a range of scale systems. Classical Greek and Roman architecture, for example, used a modular system of measurement. In classical architecture each module was the width of the column base, and this was used to determine the classical system of orders and their relative proportioning. Le Corbusier also used a modular system based on the proportions of the human body, which ensured that his architectural designs related to human scale.

To represent a space or building, comparative scale systems are needed to design, develop and explain the architectural idea. Plan, section and elevation drawings and models are the conventions used to communicate the idea, however they need to be created using a system that can be measured and is understood by the architect, builder and client alike.

When drawing to scale, the right scale system needs to be used for the appropriate context. Smaller or larger-scale investigations will lend themselves better to different types of projects, for example, the design of a city will be better understood in large scale, whereas the design of a piece of furniture will necessitate a smaller scale system and drawing.

Understanding scale is to connect with the relative size of cities, places, buildings, spaces and objects and learn how they in turn connect with one another and the people that occupy and use them.

Project: Phare Tower
Location: Paris, France
Architects: Morphosis
Date: 2006

This schematic design by architects Morphosis is a proposal for a structure in Paris. The 300 metre-high commercial building will become an iconic form in the city and the architects have use scale to as one of its distinguishing factors (the building needs to be distinctive in form to compete with the other grand projects on the Parisian skyline). This computer generated photomontage image provides a idea of the impressive scale of the proposed structure.

Images
Examples from contemporary architects and designers bring the principles under discussion to life.

Captions
Provide contextual information about each featured project and highlight the practical application of key principles.

Representational techniques

Section headings
Each chapter unit has a clear heading to allow readers to quickly locate an area of interest.

Information panels
Supporting information panels provide contextual and supplementary content, which supports the body text.

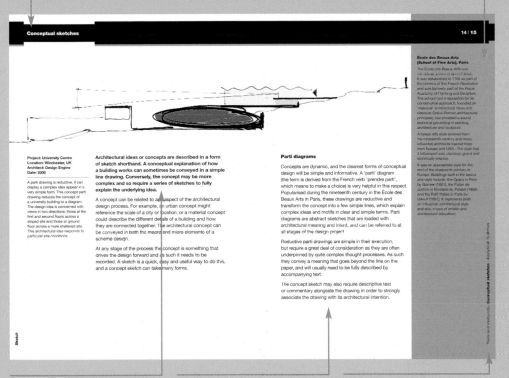

École des Beaux-Arts (School of Fine Arts), Paris

The École des Beaux-Arts was the official school of fine art in Paris. It was re-established in 1793 as part of the reforms of the French Revolution and was formerly part of the Royal Academy of Painting and Sculpture. The school had a reputation for its conservative approach, founded on 'classical' architectural ideas and classical Greco-Roman architectural principles, but provided a sound technical grounding in painting, architecture and sculpture.

A beaux arts style evolved from the nineteenth century and many influential architects trained there from Europe and USA. The style that it influenced was classical, grand and technically precise.

It was an appropriate style for the end of the nineteenth century in Europe. Buildings built in the beaux arts style include: the Opera in Paris by Garnier (1861), the Palais de Justice in Brussels by Poelart (1866) and the Petit Palais in Paris by Girault (1897). It represents both an influential architectural style and also a type of artistic and architectural education.

Project: University Centre
Location: Winchester, UK
Architect: Design Engine
Date: 2005

A parti drawing is reductive. It can display a complex idea appear in a very simple form. This concept parti drawing reduces the concept of a university building to a diagram. The design idea is concerned with views in two directions; those at the first and second floors across a sloped site and those at ground floor across a more sheltered site. This architectural idea responds to particular site conditions.

Architectural ideas or concepts are described in a form of sketch shorthand. A conceptual explanation of how a building works can sometimes be conveyed in a simple line drawing. Conversely, the concept may be more complex and so require a series of sketches to fully explain the underlying idea.

A concept can be related to any aspect of the architectural design process. For example, an urban concept might reference the scale of a city or location, or a material concept could describe the different details of a building and how they are connected together. The architectural concept can be conveyed in both the macro and micro elements of a scheme design.

At any stage of the process the concept is something that drives the design forward and as such it needs to be recorded. A sketch is a quick, easy and useful way to do this, and a concept sketch can take many forms.

Parti diagrams

Concepts are dynamic, and the clearest forms of conceptual design will be simple and informative. A 'parti' diagram (the term is derived from the French verb 'prendre parti', which means to make a choice) is very helpful in this respect. Popularised during the nineteenth century in the École des Beaux Arts in Paris, these drawings are reductive and transform the concept into a few simple lines, which explain complex ideas and motifs in clear and simple terms. Parti diagrams are abstract sketches that are loaded with architectural meaning and intent, and can be referred to at all stages of the design project.

Reductive parti drawings are simple in their execution, but require a great deal of consideration as they are often underpinned by quite complex thought processes. As such they convey a meaning that goes beyond the line on the paper, and will usually need to be fully described by accompanying text.

The concept sketch may also require descriptive text or commentary alongside the drawing in order to strongly associate the drawing with its architectural intention.

Sketch

Tools and methods: **Conceptual sketches** – Analytical sketches

Introductions
Each unit's introduction appears in bold text and outlines the concepts that are to be discussed.

Body text
In-depth discussion of working methods and best practice is covered in the book's body text.

Chapter navigation
Highlights the current chapter unit and lists the previous and following units.

How to get the most out of this book

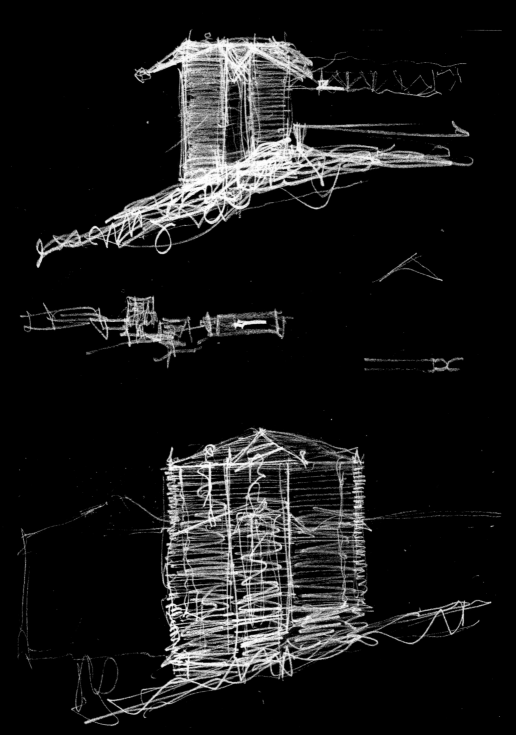

A sketch by definition is a quick, loose and open drawing. It is the speed inherent in this sort drawing that makes it a powerful way to describe an idea. Forms of sketching can range from providing a kind of visual note-taking, observing real conditions and situations, to the production of analytical drawings that deconstruct an idea or concept.

Sketches can be categorised according to concept, analysis and observation.

Conceptual sketches can reveal the essence of a complex idea. The challenge in the concept sketch is to clearly and concisely communicate the design intention. A concept sketch may be drawn at the beginning of the project, but it should still be relevant on the project's completion.

Analytical sketches can be used to analyse a building, space or component. These can be created at any stage of the design process. In a project's initial stages they may convey a design intention; later on in the design process they can explain ideas associated with journeys through the building or aspects of construction.

Observational sketches can be used to describe aspects of buildings, exploring materials or space in detail.

There are many sketching techniques that can be explored and further developed until individual preferences and a personal style are established. Stylistic variations will be in accordance with the medium used (pen, pencil, charcoal etc.); the different use and application of colour, tone or texture; the use of collage and material; the thickness or the sparseness of the line or the size and scale of image. Above all else, a personal sketching technique needs to be developed through practice and experimentation.

Project: Kielder Observatory
Location: Northumberland, UK
Architect: Hyde + Hyde
Date: 2005

The concept underlying this scheme was a homage to the cosmos. This pencil sketch shows an idea of a building as a telescope housing, opening out as a series of steel petals to reveal the sky.

The inspiration for this was a flower, with petals opening upwards and outward towards the sun. The concept sketch illustrates how the building reacts to nature in a similar fashion; it is like a piece of machinery that adapts itself and transforms to allow the view of the night sky.

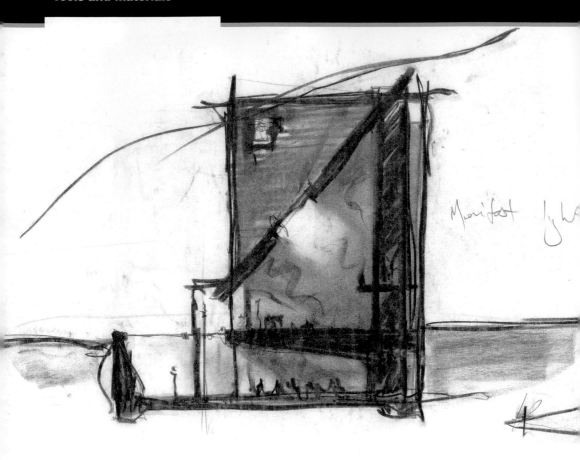

Project: Chapel of the Holy Wash
Location: Swansea, Wales
Architect: Hyde + Hyde
Date: 2002

This charcoal sketch shows the relationship between the chapel and the landscape, and also conveys the sense of sanctuary that the building offers. The use of charcoal brings an intense quality to the drawing and allows the light entering the space to be clearly understood.

Sketching requires a range of tools, and first and foremost is the sketchbook itself. When selecting a sketchbook, important factors to consider are convenience and portability and the purpose of your intended drawings. It's also important to purchase the best quality paper you can afford. Better quality paper will be more flexible as it will work equally well if sketching in pencil or pen, or if using watercolours.

An A4 (210 x 297mm) sketchbook is a good starting point, as the page is large enough to accommodate experimentation with different sketching techniques and it allows bigger images to be produced. Alternatively an A5 (148 x 210mm) sketchbook is very useful for travel because it fits neatly into a pocket and can be carried easily. An A3 (297 x 420mm) sketchbook is excellent for life and large-scale observational drawings (such as elevations).

Line hierarchy

When sketching it's an excellent idea to have a range of pens, pencils and colouring media at your disposal because the thickness of the lines in a sketch are extremely important. There is a hierarchy associated with the line and its values vary in sketching. A fine line can be used for shading and detail and a thicker, heavier line will suggest form and substance.

Different drawing media will affect the line hierarchy. Fibre-point pens, which are available in a range of nib sizes, are useful for capturing detail. Pencils can also supply a range of line weights, as well as being available in soft (B) and hard (H) leads. Using varied pencil types will allow a range of differently styled sketches to be developed. A 0.5mm propelling pencil, with a range of hard and soft leads, is another versatile drawing tool.

Sketching with a black ink pen is an important skill to develop because the contrast that the ink line, produce against the paper, and the permanency of the line, produce a 'definite' image.

One tool that probably isn't necessary is an eraser. When sketching, practice is all important and even the mistakes can be beneficial, so it makes sense not to rub them out! Remember, a sketchbook is a collection of drawings and reflects the development of techniques and ideas.

Tools for architectural drawing

To enjoy sketching, and achieve a range of results, it is important to have different sorts of equipment to experiment with. Simple drawings can be produced with a single sheet of paper and a pencil. Then, by further considering the type of pencil and the type of paper, the possible variations are endless. With each drawing, experiment with a new tool or medium. Listed below is a range of equipment that can help you vary and further your drawing experiences.

Mechanical pencils (0.3 or 0.5mm)
Fibre-tip pens (0.2, 0.5, 0.8mm)
Adjustable set square (20cm)
45 degree set square
60 degree set square
Circle template
30cm scale rule
Roll of white tracing paper
Roll of detail paper
A3 tracing pad (60gsm)
A3 film pad (50micron)
Drawing board
Sketchbook
Tape measure
Set of French curves

Tools and materials › Conceptual sketches

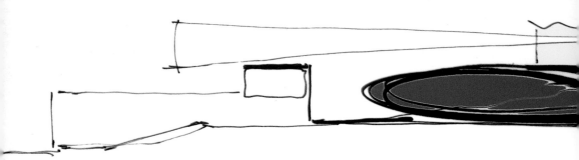

**Project: University Centre
Location: Winchester, UK
Architect: Design Engine
Date: 2005**

A parti drawing is reductive, it can
display a complex idea in a very
simple form. This concept parti
drawing reduces the concept of
a university building to a diagram.
The design idea is concerned with
views in two directions; those at the
first and second floors across a
sloped site and those at ground
floor across a more sheltered site.
This architectural idea responds to
particular site conditions.

**Architectural ideas or concepts are described in a form
of sketch shorthand. A conceptual explanation of how
a building works can sometimes be conveyed in a simple
line drawing. Conversely, the concept may be more
complex and so require a series of sketches to fully
explain the underlying idea.**

A concept can be related to any aspect of the architectural
design process. For example, an urban concept might
reference the scale of a city or location, or a material concept
could describe the different details of a building and how
they are connected together. The architectural concept can
be conveyed in both the macro and micro elements of a
scheme design.

At any stage of the process the concept is something that
drives the design forward and as such it needs to be
recorded. A sketch is a quick, easy and useful way to do this,
and a concept sketch can take many forms.

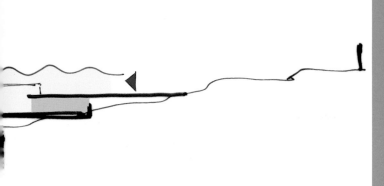

**École des Beaux-Arts
(School of Fine Arts), Paris**

The École des Beaux-Arts was
the official school of art in France.
It was established in 1793 as part of
the reforms of the French Revolution
and was formerly part of the Royal
Academy of Painting and Sculpture.
The school had a reputation for its
conservative approach, founded on
'classical' architectural ideas and
classical Greco-Roman architectural
principles, but provided a sound
technical grounding in painting,
architecture and sculpture.

A beaux-arts style evolved from
the nineteenth century and many
influential architects trained there
from Europe and USA. The style that
it influenced was classical, grand and
technically precise.

It was an appropriate style for the
end of the nineteenth century in
Europe. Buildings built in the beaux-
arts style include the Paris Opéra
by Garnier (1861), the Palais de
Justice in Brussels by Poelaert (1866)
and the Petit Palais in Paris by
Girault (1897). It represents both
an influential architectural style
and also a type of artistic and
architectural education.

Parti diagrams

Concepts are dynamic, and the clearest forms of conceptual
design will be simple and informative. A 'parti' diagram
(the term is derived from the French verb 'prendre parti',
which means to make a choice) is very helpful in this respect.
Popularised during the nineteenth century in the École des
Beaux-Arts in Paris, these drawings are reductive and
transform the concept into a few simple lines, which explain
complex ideas and motifs in clear and simple terms.
Parti diagrams are abstract sketches that are loaded with
architectural meaning and intent, and can be referred to at
all stages of the design project.

Reductive parti drawings are simple in their execution,
but require a great deal of consideration as they are often
underpinned by quite complex thought processes. As such
they convey a meaning that goes beyond the line on the
paper, and will usually need to be fully described by
accompanying text.

The concept sketch may also require descriptive text
or commentary alongside the drawing in order to strongly
associate the drawing with its architectural intention.

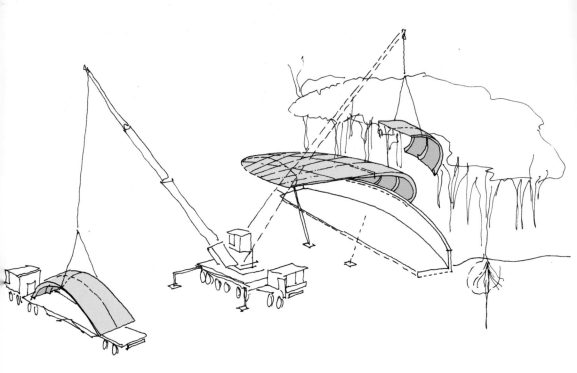

**Project: The Visitor Centre,
Hardwick Park
Location: Durham, UK
Architect: Design Engine
Date: 2006**

These images describe a
construction process for a
prefabricated project. The image
is drawn as a perspective sketch
to explain the removal of the
prefabricated elements from a
truck and details how they will be
fixed into place on a hard-to-access
site. The drawing is self-explanatory
and needs no accompanying text,
it simply describes a process of
assembly and construction.

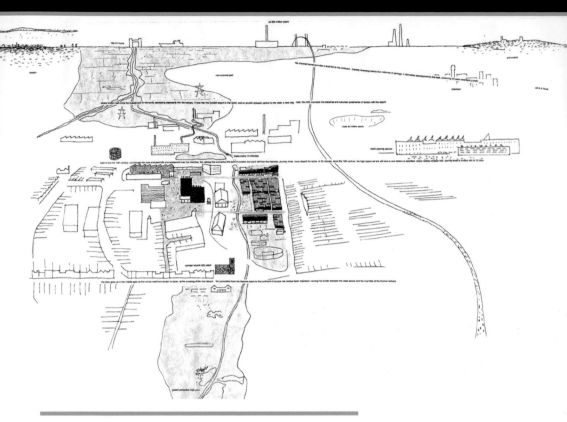

The old fencing school
(c. seventeenth century)

The Globe Theatre
(c. seventeenth century)

Theatrum Gedanense
(twenty-first century interpretation)

Project: Theatrum Gedanense
(left)
Location: Gdansk, Poland
Architect: Design Engine
Date: 2004

These sketches are not created to a particular scale, but using simple shapes they explain the idea of the Theatrum Gedanense's roof by referencing other building forms, including a fencing school and another theatre design. The design proposes a roof that can be both open and closed, creating a flexible use of the space to produce an open-air theatre and an arena.

Project: Dartford Town Centre
(above)
Location: Dartford, UK
Architect: Witherford Watson Mann
Date: 1998

This is a bird's eye perspective sketch of a proposal for a town centre design. In this sketch it is possible to see that the east–west road and rail infrastructures are flattened and used as a series of horizons, with the River Thames at the top of the sketch and the River Darent running through it. The balance of the proposal's volumes, public spaces and landscapes are shown in this drawing in the context of their metropolitan and landscape setting.

Tools and materials › **Conceptual sketches** › Analytical sketches

Analysis of an idea requires a way of thinking that separates, simplifies and clarifies. An analytical sketch usually follows the same working principles, and as such is a device that can help explain complex aspects of architecture.

Analytical drawings can be used to isolate specific aspects of an architectural idea, and describe them as a series of parts or components. So, for example, analytical drawings could be used technically to describe the structural system of a building, or equally take an environmental approach and describe how sunlight moves through a space, or they may even describe a building's construction or assembly system. When designing building systems, architects will use analytical sketches to work through their ideas and develop particular responses that will shape their overall design approach.

The analysis of an idea needs to be logical and easy to understand. The drawings that first begin the process of an architectural design are site analysis sketches. Whether these analyse a building, an urban site or a landscape, these drawings describe what already exists – whether it be an aspect of the local environmental conditions, or the type of materials used on the site, or a reference to a previous event – as a series of critical diagrams. These analytical diagrams separate ideas that will inform and influence the subsequent architectural design.

Using analytical sketches to record site information produces a map of the site's building forms, histories and its topography, which combine to create a full picture of the site conditions. They will reference aspects of the site that can be described 'as is', in the present, and 'as was', in the past. Analytical sketches are effectively a form of on-site note-taking.

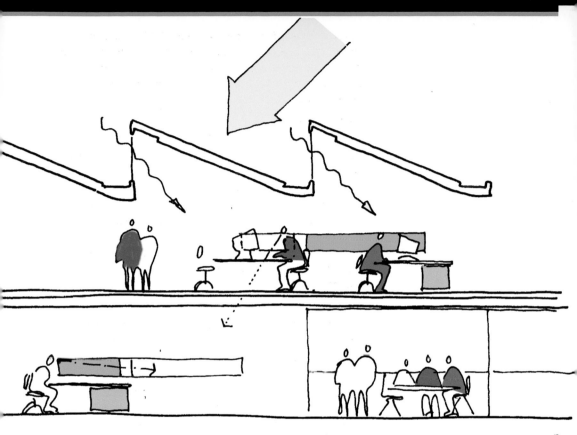

Project: Giffords Head Office
Location: Hampshire, UK
Architects: Design Engine
Date: 2004

Part of the challenge of this design for the head office building of an engineering firm was to create a 'deep' plan to the building, whilst still achieving as much natural daylight as possible. This sketch analyses how the building's design will work with natural light and explains how direct light is prevented from reaching employees' desktops and computer screens, but allows indirect light to enter the building via a carefully designed rooflight system.

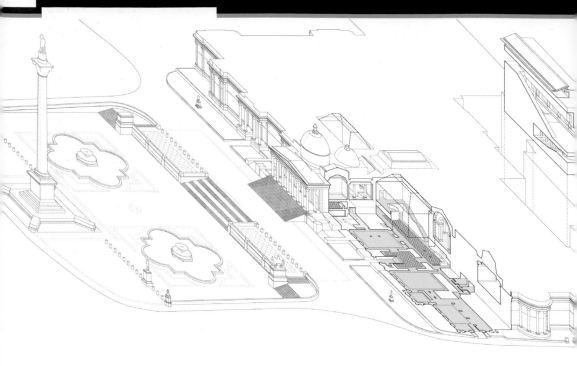

Project: The National Portrait Gallery
Location: London, UK
Architect: Dixon Jones
Date: 1997

This drawing shows a proposed relationship between Trafalgar Square, The National Gallery and The National Portrait Gallery, creating a new view of the existing buildings. The architect wanted to explore the possibility of looking over the top of the existing buildings that frame Trafalgar Square. The architectural idea used an escalator to take visitors from the ground floor up to a level where the view south across London was framed by a new window in a restaurant.

The drawing encapsulates the thinking behind the architectural idea; creating it required a conceptual understanding of the city and a series of public spaces as well as the architectural design for the gallery.

Conceptual field

As well as being used at the beginning of the design process, as the scheme of a building further develops, many of the architectural drawings produced are analytical (even the detail drawings that explain the assembly of a building are themselves a form of analysis).

For example, analytical sketches can be used to explain site interpretation, any structural and environmental ideas for the site as well as detailed construction and assembly ideas. Cities can also be described through analytical drawing or mapping, and doing so often reduces complex forms of urban design to simple diagrams and sketches.

A series of analytical sketches will describe the thinking and evolution of the design idea, deconstructing it into stages of development and understanding. These sketches will reveal the thinking of the architect or designer and (when compared to the realised building) how it has influenced the final architectural scheme.

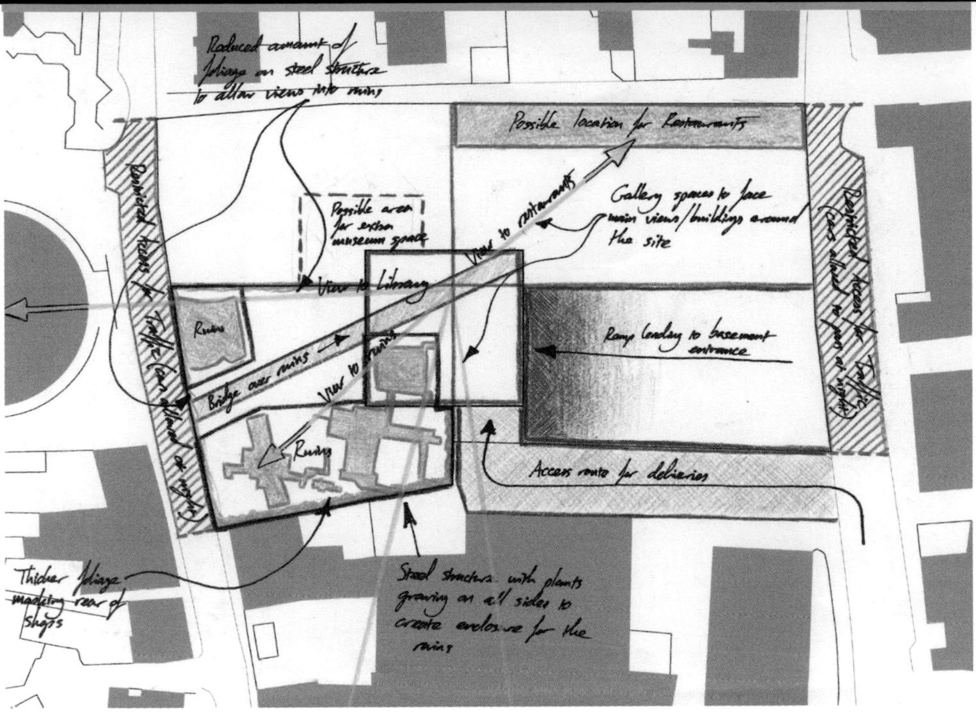
Reduced amount of foliage on steel structure to allow views into ruins
Possible location for Restaurants
Gallery spaces to face main views/buildings around the site
Possible area for extra museum space
View to restaurants
View to Library
Ruins
Bridge over ruins
View to ruins
Ramp leading to basement entrance
Restricted Access for Traffic (cars allowed at night)
Restricted Access for Traffic (cars allowed to pass at night)
Ruins
Access route for deliveries
Thicker foliage masking rear of shops
Steel structure with plants growing on all sides to create enclosure for the ruins

Project: Chichester Museum
Location: Chichester, UK
Designer: Paul Craven Bartle
Date: 2007

This sketch is created over a site plan to analyse aspects of route for pedestrians and cars. It also displays the site's boundaries, definitions and historical layers. To create this kind of analysis an understanding of the historical evolution of the site is needed and the site needs to be studied over a period of time to record journeys across, over and through the site. This one drawing pulls together both types of information and presents it in one easy-to-read map.

Project: Observational sketch
Location: Chichester, UK
Designer: Paul Craven Bartle
Date: 2007

This observational sketch is a perspective view, but it also describes the scale and the massing of the buildings in the street. The use of watercolours suggests the colours and textures of the building materials and the context of the street. Placing outlines of figures in the foreground of the drawing provides the sketch with a sense of scale.

Observational drawing is an important part of the design process. Careful observation allows us to first absorb and then comprehend what we see. To represent this in a drawing is a learned skill.

To produce an observational drawing first requires an initial period of concentration and analysis. It is important to take the time to really 'see'. Look carefully at the subject; if it is a street scene or building look at it in terms of its underlying structure or layout as this will help allow a 'plan' to be established for the drawing. Before you put pen to paper consider how your drawing sits on the page and what techniques you will use to render or colour the image. The composition of the observational image on the page is key.

Project: Travel sketch
Location: Venice, Italy
Designer: Jeremy Davies
Date: 2006

As well as capturing the space within and buildings surrounding St Marks Square (in the Italian city of Venice) in great detail, this observational sketch also captures the activities within, and use of, the area. This travel sketch captures the city's famous annual carnival, when the city's residents parade in colourful masks and vibrant costumes. As much as the buildings, the detail of the people and their costumes explain the place. The buildings are a defining background to the sketch.

Framing the sketch

To construct a good observational sketch, visualise the entire view and 'frame' your subject so that it becomes a separate image from everything around it. Deciding what is important about your sketch, for example, determining those elements of the view that will form the focus of your drawing, is crucial.

Use guidelines to establish your framework. These guides may be a horizontal or vertical axis or other form of reference line on the page. Squares, circles or other geometric figures can also be used as guides and will help regularise your sketch. By gradually laying these guides on the paper you will be able to organise and place your view and in doing so help your drawing develop.

When the framework for the sketch has been established, it serves as an outline for the view. Take the time to check that this outline is correct. It may need to be adjusted to get the proportion and distances right.

Once the framework is correctly established, more line layers can be incorporated to develop detail in the drawing. At each point of addition the accuracy needs to be checked in order to ensure that the observational integrity of the drawing remains intact. Once all the lines are in place, tone, texture and colour can all be added to the sketch. It is important to 'build' drawings in this way, so that each stage is clear and if there are difficulties with proportion, scale or detail the image can be modified accordingly, again to keep the representation 'true'.

Analytical sketches › **Observational sketches** › Sketchbooks

Sketchbooks are containers of design information and can take many forms in order to suit different ways of thinking. Sometimes they serve as a kind of 'aide-mémoire' to help record and pinpoint specific details, or they can be used to track the broader development process of a scheme.

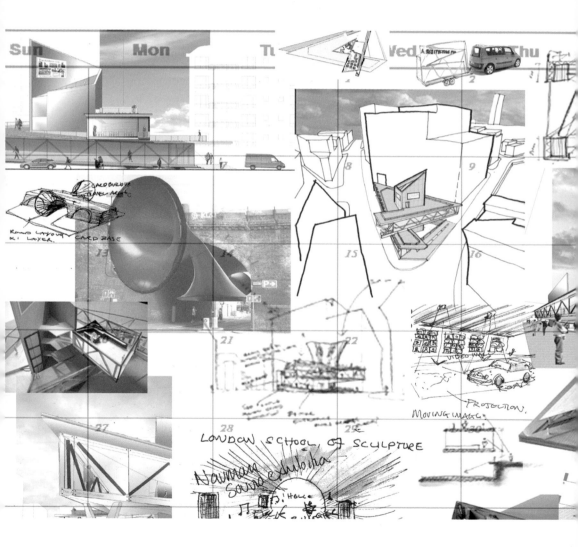

Design diaries

A design diary is a sketchbook that is updated daily with thoughts, references and ideas. As the name suggests, the key point here is that it is treated like a diary and is personal, honest and complete. Some ideas in a design diary will be quickly recorded and never referred to again, while others will have more value and be reworked, developed and enhanced.

By virtue of its nature, a design diary collects ideas and drawings chronologically. Doing so allows concepts to be referenced over time and provides a record of how a project develops and evolves. At certain points it may be necessary to pause, reflect and reconsider the design direction. A design diary allows the process of the project to be traced back as a lineage of design development.

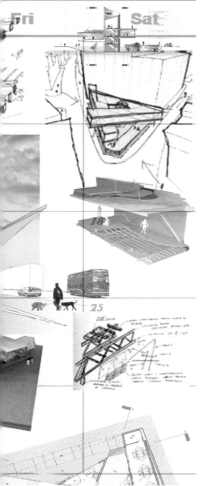

Project: Design diary
Designer: Adam Heike
Date: 2005

This page from a student design diary has composite images created from overlaid sketches, models and drawings of a design proposal. The images also contain research references. The range of different photographs and sketches explain the thinking behind the architectural idea and have been collaged together to create an overview of the idea's development.

Research sketchbooks

A research sketchbook is a collection of ideas and references surrounding a particular aspect of the design concept (for example, the use of a particular material within the scheme), allowing the element to be investigated, developed and shaped into its final form. The research may be recorded as notes, photographs, photocopies or web images, as well as sketches.

A research notebook will usually contain the results of research and investigation that are beyond the scope of the project in question. This means that research sketchbooks are a useful resource and can suggest new ideas for application in other contexts. For example, a particular building material or process that is thought to be relevant in one scheme may ultimately prove to be unsuitable. However, it could contribute to a future project or idea. This means that all investigations in research sketchbooks are valid and so it is crucial to record and archive them.

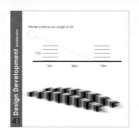

Project: Research sketchbook
Designer: Sian Crookes
Date: 2006

These pages from a research notebook describe areas of investigation for a design project, some are at the scale of the city, while others are investigations of materials and details. The images include precedents that have informed the design idea as well as detail references and investigations of materials and their application in the architectural project.

Travel sketchbooks

Travel sketchbooks are specific to a particular journey or experience. They can be used to represent a range of observations about a place or culture. Architects who keep travel sketchbooks may use them to refer back to specific architectural ideas encountered on their travels and reconsider them with their own design projects in mind. Such ideas may include a particular use of materials, a specific type of structure or a particular experience of light affecting a room or a space.

Travel sketches tend to be both observational (describing what is seen) and analytical (analysing through diagram and ideas and concepts of design).

Developing personal preferences, approaches and styles is an important aspect of sketching. These can be established through experimentation with drawing styles, techniques, materials or media. If you see a drawing that you like, find out what materials were used to construct it and then adopt, adapt and experiment to develop your own individual approach.

Mixing media from a range of different sources can be another way to find out what works for you. Different areas of art and design, from illustration and animation to graphic design and fine art, use different representation techniques that can be adapted for architectural drawing and presentation.

Experimental sketching

At the initial stages of a design, the idea can move quickly, so the drawings need to keep pace with it. At these points is can be useful and appropriate to draw quick, intuitive lines, a spontaneous type of drawing, to get the idea down on paper. Exploratory sketches need to be more considered; these sort of crafted drawings are used to work through a particular problem, or develop a drawn presentation to explain a scheme.

Sketches don't always have to fall into one of these three neat 'types', though. For example, sketching what we see can be juxtaposed with more abstract drawings. This can be achieved using diagrams and annotated drawings that explore an imagined idea. Sketches can also be moved from one drawing environment to another. A sketch can be scanned into a computer, and further developed with CAD software (see page134–139) to become a hybrid drawing that is both freehand and computer generated. Moving between different drawing platforms like this creates diversity in the sketch and personalises it even more.

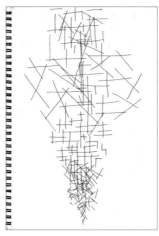

Project: Experimental sketch
Designer: Edward Steed
Date: 2007

This sketch represents a space as a series of lines that describe movements or journeys across and through the space; one sketch is white chalk lines on black paper, the other contrasts, using black ink on white paper. These two images are an impression of the same space, the different use of paper and line create different impressions of the space that can be read simultaneously.

Project: Experimental sketch
Designer: Edward Steed
Date: 2007

This series of investigations of a space uses photo images that are traced over. Paper is laid on top of images to create a collage effect, tracing lines of movement through a room.

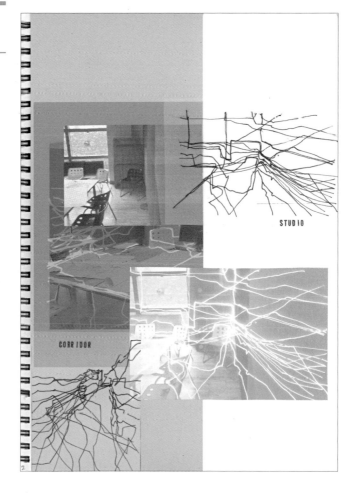

STUDIO

CORRIDOR

Sketchbooks › **Experimental techniques** › Exercise 1: sketch

Materials and media

Using a black pen on white paper is the traditional sketching approach that architects take, but experimenting with chalk or a white pen on black paper creates an interesting reverse contrast.

Using different type and width of pencil lead will also change the dynamic of the drawing; a thick piece of graphite can strike bold lines across pieces of paper, whereas a thinner 0.3mm pencil lead will create more refined controlled lines.

Using watercolours or coloured pencils when sketching can highlight various aspects of the drawing. Watercolours have an added advantage as they can be layered. The first layer can be transparent to give a wash across the page, and subsequent layers of colour can be added to provide more depth to the image.

Other techniques

Collage (see pages 112–113) lends an image real texture. A collage image may start as a series of disjointed pieces, which are then carefully organised and placed to create a new composite view of a design idea. The choice of materials for a collage image is important: they may complement one another or be selected to create a deliberate contrast.

In the context of architectural representational techniques, photomontage (see pages 112–113) combines an existing site photograph with a sketch of an architectural idea or proposal, creating a composite image that offers a realistic impression of a future architecture. In this sort of image other elements can be added to lend it a sense of scale. In particular, adding figures and vehicles can provide a sense of scale that is universally recognised, and can also imply the types of activities and events that are associated with the architectural idea.

Concept
aashaven
anism, European Cities
403
007
my Davies

Project: Student housing proposal
Location: Rotterdam,
the Netherlands
Designer: Jeremy Davies
Date: 2007

This is an external perspective of
a proposal for a student housing
scheme in Rotterdam. The
perspective uses a collage technique
to create an effect of the skyline and
city beyond. Figures have been
included to give the image a sense
of scale and reality.

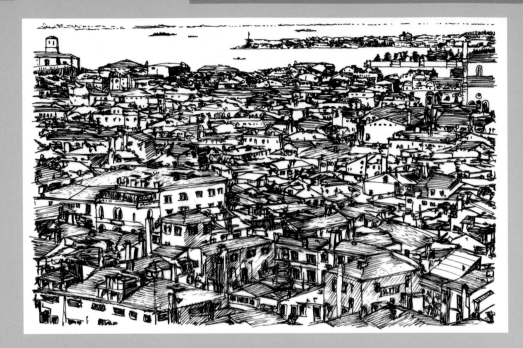

Project: Serial Vision
(above and facing page)
Location: Venice, Italy
Designer: Jeremy Davies
Date: 2006

These three sketches are part of a series of sketches taken on a journey through Venice, to describe a sequence of experiences of the city. They connect to a particular journey, and interpret a personal impression of Venice.

Sketching is something that needs to be practised in order for your technique to improve and develop. Observation is important, as is taking the time to think about what you are drawing.

Everyday experiences can be rediscovered through drawing them. Sketching journeys around a city or a building, framing experiences and views, and relating these to particular spaces or rooms in a building is a very personal method for observing and describing architectural ideas.

In his book *The Concise Townscape* (Architectural Press, 1994), Gordon Cullen advocates a sketching technique called 'serial views'. This analysis involves drawing a journey around a city first as a map and then as a series of connected views. What is ultimately achieved by doing so is a personal description of the journey. Serial views is a technique that can equally be applied to journeys through spaces and buildings as well as cities.

Serial views

This exercise will teach you how to observe a space and draw your journey through it in such as way that it captures and conveys your own understanding and experiences en route.

1   Take a journey through a large building that you enjoy visiting, such as a library, gallery or museum.

2   While en route, identify a series of spaces that you think are interesting and communicate your experience of the building.

3   Sketch the plan of this journey. The plan should occupy at least one page of your sketchbook. This exercise is not about drawing to scale; the plan can be a loose, informal diagram of the connected spaces.

4   Divide another page of your sketchbook into six parts. On your sketch plan identify six key points of your experience of the building, number these points and draw six corresponding sketch perspectives to describe your journey.

This exercise is all about practice, so draw freehand. Don't rub drawings out either – draw lightly at first and then make the line more definite when you are confident.

Use colour to enhance the sketches. Highlighting a particular feature, such as the use of a particular material or a detail that attracts your attention, will start to personalise your drawing and so emphasise your particular interest in the view.

Experimental techniques › Exercise 1: sketch

Representational techniques

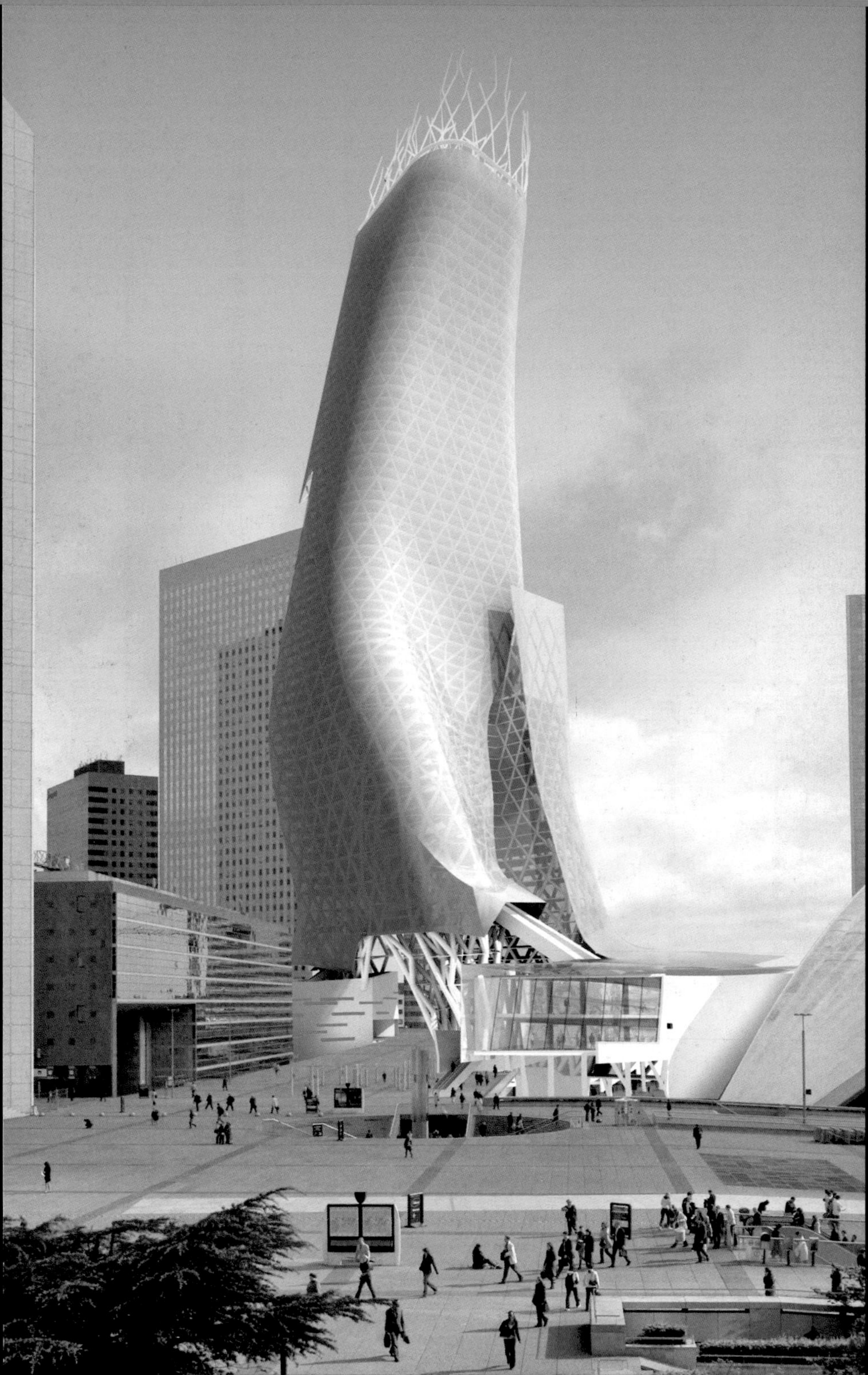

Scale has multiple meanings in architecture. Drawings can be to scale (adhering to an established or agreed reference or system), 'out of', or 'not to' scale. Historically, architects have employed a range of scale systems. Classical Greek and Roman architecture, for example, used a modular system of measurement. In classical architecture each module was the width of the column base, and this was used to determine the classical system of orders and their relative proportioning. Le Corbusier also used a modular system based on the proportions of the human body, which ensured that his architectural designs related to human scale.

To represent a space or building, comparative scale systems are needed to design, develop and explain the architectural idea. Plan, section and elevation drawings and models are the conventions used to communicate the idea; however, they need to be created using a system that can be measured and is understood by the architect, builder and client alike.

When drawing to scale, the right scale system needs to be used for the appropriate context. Smaller or larger scale investigations will lend themselves better to different types of projects, for example, the design of a city will be better understood in large scale, whereas the design of a piece of furniture will necessitate a smaller scale system and drawing.

Understanding scale is to connect with the relative size of cities, places, buildings, spaces and objects and to learn how they in turn connect with one another and the people that occupy and use them.

Project: Phare Tower
Location: Paris, France
Architect: Morphosis
Date: 2006

This schematic design by architects Morphosis is a proposal for a structure in the Parisian district of La Défense. The Phare Tower is a 300 metre-high commercial building that is scheduled for completion in 2012. This computer-generated photomontage image provides an idea of the impressive scale of the proposed structure, which is set to become an iconic form in the city.

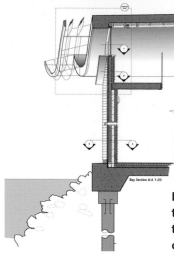

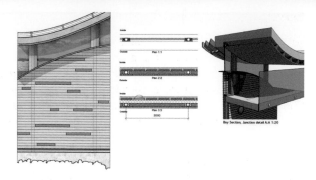

Bay Section A:A 1:20

Plan 1:1

Plan 2:2

Plan 3:3
2000

Bay Section, Junction detail A:A 1:20

Project: Emsworth Activity Centre
Location: Emsworth, UK
Designer: Rocky Marchant
Date: 2006

These drawings describe a section of a building that is located on an exposed seaside site. The drawings comprise of a section, elevation, plans and perspective image. There is sufficient detail in the drawings to understand the size and dimensions of the materials used in the external cladding of the building.

Buildings can be quantitatively described by measuring them in different ways, for example, by quantifying the amounts of materials required to build them, or by understanding the size of their internal and external spaces.

Measuring existing buildings is important when there is an intention to extend, renovate or redevelop a structure, as it allows the architect to suggest how best to respond to various openings in walls, floors and roofs. There is also much to be learned from studying and measuring an existing building; doing so can provide an understanding of how it has been put together, what materials have been used, or particular details of its construction. To take a building and explore it via the plan, section and elevation details will explain many aspects of the original design concept.

Measurement systems

Measuring systems are universally agreed or understood. Today we commonly use metric or imperial systems of measurement. The metric system uses millimetres (mm), centimetres (cm), metres (m) and kilometres (kms) as its basic units of measurement and the imperial system uses units of inches (in), feet (ft), yards (yd) and miles (mi).

In addition to these standard conventions, modular systems use an understood 'module' as their basic unit of measurement. For example, in Classical architecture the understood module was the width of the base of the column. Le Corbusier's 'Le Modulor' (1948) divided the body into units and his architectural drawings related to this system of measurement (see page 35).

Survey

To better understand how measurements in architecture work, buildings and spaces that already exist can be measured and drawn. When an existing space is measured and reproduced as a drawing it is referred to as a 'survey'. Surveys are normally drawn to record the conditions of a space so that the architect can respond to them accordingly.

A site survey will consist of plans that explain the site's boundaries and section drawings that will describe the site's landscape and any important surrounding features. The different site levels will be indicated as map contours or as a series of spot heights that show the relative height of each.

Information about the site and its boundaries can be mapped digitally from a number of online providers. For a fee, any site plan available on the database can be downloaded, printed and used as a basis for a CAD drawing (subject to certain copyright rules). These websites have facilitated an easier connection of a design idea with a site because the digital map can be imported into a CAD drawing at any scale.

Measured dimensioned drawings

It is usual to apply numerical dimensions to measured drawings, as this allows the information to be read accurately and easily. These dimensions may be displayed as a series of individual measurements or as a running dimension.

When undertaking a survey, it is important to measure the spaces individually and then incorporate other dimensions that measure the overall space or building (as these act as a 'check' to ensure that all measurements add up correctly).

Drawing scale ratio

Architects and spatial designers tend to have a range of scales that respond to the design of the various spaces that they are engaged with.

Scale	Drawing use
1:1	Full (or real) size for details
1:2	Details
1:5	Details
1:10	Interior spaces/furniture
1:20	Interior spaces/furniture
1:50	Interior spaces/ detailed floor plans/ different floor levels
1:100	Building plans/layouts
1:500	Building layouts/ site plans
1:1000	Urban scale for site or location plans
1:1250	Site plans
1:2500	Site plans/city maps
NTS	Not to scale (abstract)

Measuring | Full size

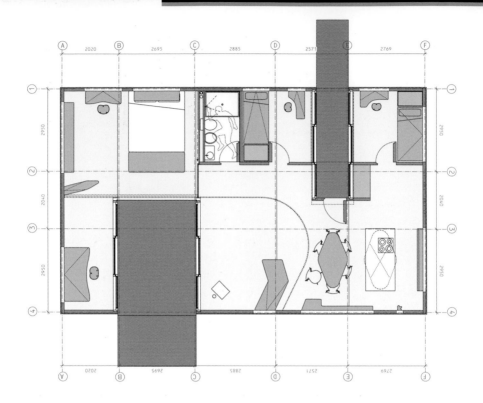

Project: Naked House
Location: Oslo, Norway
Architect: dRMM
Dates: 2006

The Naked House is a sustainable, affordable, CO_2 responsible, prefabricated timber house that can be customised to suit individual users. Conceptually, the house works as a cut-out diagram, with all numbered elements (including door and window openings) digitally pre-cut from substantial cross-laminated timber panels.

This set of Naked House drawings includes dimensioned plan and sections. The plan drawing has a clear set of measurements related to an organisational grid. As this is a 'flat pack' kit, the dimensions are critical to understand the assembly of the house.

Equipment

In order to obtain and record precise measurements in a scale drawing, calibrated equipment is needed. The most basic scale-drawing tool is a scale rule, which is specifically dimensioned to give precise measurements.

Different sorts of designers will use different sorts of scale rules. For example, an engineer and a product designer will use different scale systems as references in their design work and so will need to use different types of scale rule that work within these systems to record the measurements.

SECTION A-A

When surveying spaces, a tape measure is a basic, but essential, piece of equipment. Tape measures are available in a variety of sizes and again the most suitable size will depend on the scale of the object or space to be measured. For example, a three-metre tape measure is useful for small-dimensioned spaces and objects, but if measuring a building it will be useless and a 30-metre tape will suit this purpose far better. In addition to traditional tape measures, digital devices will accurately measure a room or building using laser beam technology.

To understand the different levels across a site, a theodolite is necessary. A theodolite is an instrument with a rolling telescope that is used for measuring both horizontal and vertical angles. It will be placed at a particular point on a site to create an ordnance datum for the site, from that point all levels can be described relative to that datum. A large site can have a considerable range of levels, and this can affect the subsequent design or scheme layout.

A building proposal can sometimes benefit from full-size exploration. Renaissance architects favoured this technique and often made full-size representations of elements of proposed buildings (such as their dome or cupola structure) to give an impression of a new building form. In cases of specialised construction, it may be that a component needs to be made at full size to ensure that it will fit its intended context. Or there may be a need for experimentation; a particular element of the architectural scheme may need to be tested as a full-size piece (in the same way that a prototype may be constructed in product design or engineering) to ensure that it works properly. There may also be innovative aspects of the design scheme that need to be built at full size in order to be properly understood.

Full-size staging, drawing and modelling

Some spaces can be 'staged' to suggest a building or object in context. The use of disposable materials such as cardboard or polystyrene can create an impression of the intended design at full size and so allow a better understanding of its impact within a space. Such pieces can also be read as installations: as full-size pieces of sculpture in a space.

Generally, drawing or modelling at fullsize will be restricted to architectural details (such as a door handle or a piece of furniture, for example, see pages 42–43), where the type, texture and tactility of the materials used are important design considerations, or to specific fixing details that need to be developed from particular components, made full size and tested as a prototype.

**Project: The Architecture
Foundation Summer House
Location: London, UK
Architects: 6a architects and
Eley Kishimoto
Date: 2005**

Designed by 6a Architects and
fashion designers Eley Kishimoto
the Summer House explores the
potential for using pattern in
architecture, and it created a
temporary public space and
landmark for two months during
summer 2005. The outside was clad
with plywood laser cut with Eley
Kishimoto's pattern of Rapunzel's
hair, allowing dappled light into the
interior of the tower. At night, the
tower was lit from within to glow like
a giant lantern. This project was
modelled initially to scale and was
effectively a full-size installation
constructed in an existing space
using panels of plywood, much like a
set element for a theatre stage.

Virtually full size

For most architecture, it is only at the point when the concept
is finally constructed that there can be a 'real' understanding
of the full-scale impact of the building's form, materiality and
scale. However, advances in technology now mean that it's
possible for a proposed form to be virtually tested in its
surroundings.

This technology has been developed in tandem with the
computer gaming industry, and allows the architect to
develop their virtual spaces, rooms, cities and environments
and suggest how we (or the user) may interact with their
ideas.

By using specialised equipment, one can virtually experience
a proposed space at full size. This can be an impressive
experience, transporting you to a world where you can open
virtual doors and move through imagined spaces. The
boundaries between architectural vision and reality are now
being challenged.

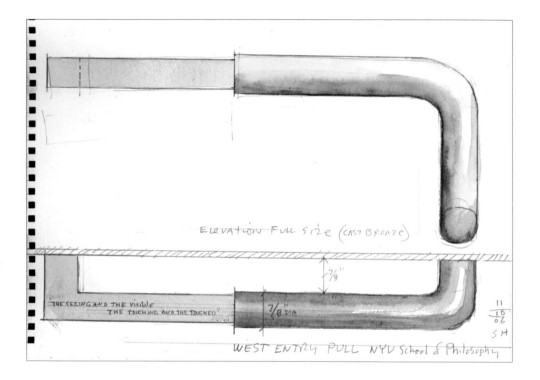

ELEVATION FULL SIZE (CAST BRONZE)

7/8"

THE SEEING AND THE VISIBLE
THE TOUCHING AND THE TOUCHED"

7/8" DIA

11
10
06

S H

WEST ENTRY PULL NYU School of Philosophy

Always design a thing by considering it in its next larger context – a chair in a room, a room in a house, a house in an environment, an environment in a city plan.

Eliel Saarinen

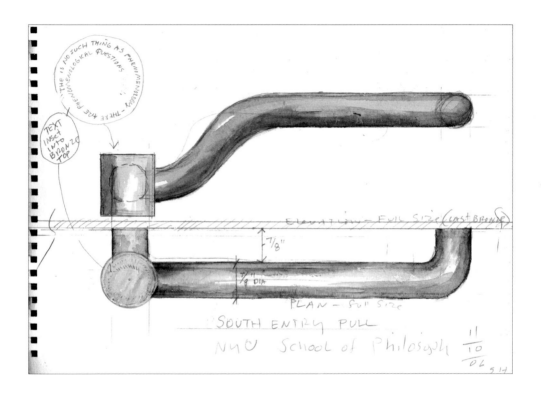

Project: Door handle, NYU School of Philosophy
Location: New York, USA
Architect: Stephen Holl Architects
Date: 2006

These watercolour drawings are a full-size representation of a door handle. Drawing something full size allows it to be understood in terms of material and scale.

Detailed scale drawings allow an in-depth investigation of a building or space through close inspection of its proposed component parts. These drawings are usually composed at scales of 1:2 (half full size), 1:5 (a fifth full size) or 1:10 (a tenth full size). Detail drawings will form part of the 'full set' of information about the proposed architecture and will relate to other drawings and information in the scheme design. This full set of drawings then describes a building from site and location through to material detail and finish.

In any given building, some details are generic and will apply throughout using standard building and construction techniques and materials, but there will also be more specialised details and these need to be designed and developed to respond to particular and perhaps unique conditions of the building.

Detail drawings

When creating a package of detail drawings, each detail needs to be considered in relationship to the whole building; the concept of the whole scheme should be visible in each of the detail drawings. It is, for example, the touch of a door handle or the relationship between a wall and a floor that, when the building is inhabited, has the most impact on our personal experience of the architecture. The approach to designing these sorts of details needs to have the same rigour as the design of the building's plan and section. The detail drawings represent the subtlety of the architectural idea and provide an understanding of how materials can come together in a way that is sympathetic to the concept.

When a building is being constructed on site, the detail drawings can be modified as the construction progresses (if need be) to respond to issues on site, varying material availability or changes in the design. Detail drawings usually contain clear written information. This text is usually supplied as an accompanying key, legend or numbered reference that explains the materials.

Assembly drawings

Assembly drawings are mechanical and engineering forms of representation that explore the 'assembly' of different component parts. These drawings are often standard instructions that suggest a uniform approach to putting materials together. This approach will be informed by manufacturer's information and guidelines about their products. In many cases these details are further developed by the architect to suit specific conditions of a building.

Details of a building's assembly and construction need to be explored at a range of scales. For example, the scale of understanding needs to allow expression of fixings such as nuts, bolts and screws. To describe this clearly, drawing scales of 1:2 and 1:5 need to be employed.

Project: Centaur Street housing
Location: London, UK
Architect: dRMM
Dates: 2004–2005

This photo of the finished Centaur Street scheme shows us the building's curving clad elevation. The scheme consisted of four split-level apartments each with their own private balcony. An apartment building situated 30m from the Eurostar viaduct may seem unlikely, but dRMM were commissioned to design a scheme based on a new housing typology for brownfield sites in London. Their scheme was a hybrid of the European horizontal apartment and the English vertical terrace house.

Each apartment enjoys a generous interior that is organised as a large, open, double-height living space, interpenetrated by adjacent enclosed bedrooms and stairs, which form a concrete buffer to the railway.

Full size › **Detail scale** › Interior scale

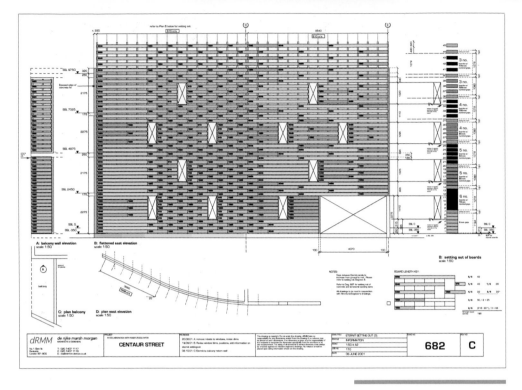

Project: Centaur Street housing
Location: London, UK
Architect: dRMM
Dates: 2004–2005

This drawing (above) sets out the building's curved elevation. It enabled the designer to create a detailed study for the cladding of the complex curved façade and was also used to help explain how they intended the building to be built.

The assembly detail drawings (right) show sections of key details at 1:5 scale. All of the plans are cross referenced to the 1:20 sections.

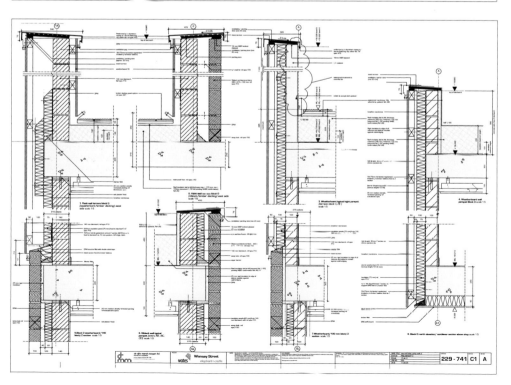

Project: The Eco-Station
Location: Various sites in the UK
Architects: David Yearley, Lorraine
Farrelly, Matt Mardell, Alex Wood
and Architecture Plb
Date: 2007

The eco-station was designed as
part of National Architecture Week
(2007) as a structure to engage the
public with the concept of
sustainability. It was designed as a
series of frames that could be easily
assembled and taken apart in a
range of locations. It was then clad
with panels using materials from
recycled mobile phones to old
plastic pipes. These detail drawings
show the scale of the project and
illustrate the plan and section
information of the structure.

Detail section drawings

A section drawing will display the internal structure of a
building (or space) as if it has been cut through vertically
or horizontally. A detailed section drawing can show the
relationship between the critical details within the sectional
planes. A section through an external wall, for example, can
describe its relationship with the building's foundation, its
floors and its roof.

These drawings are most often produced at scales of 1:10
or 1:20 depending on the size of the building. Detail section
drawings are cross-referenced to the relevant section
drawing so that the context of the detail can be understood
in relation to the rest of the building.

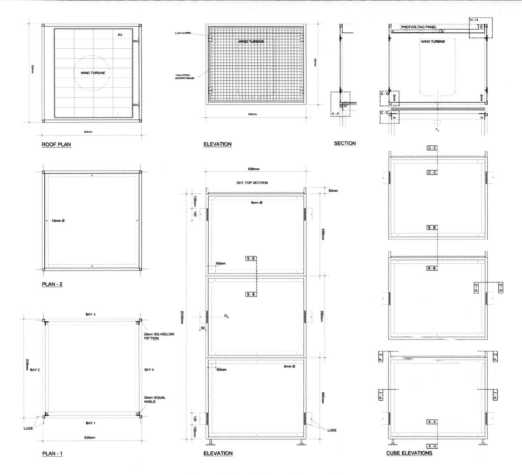

ROOF PLAN

ELEVATION

SECTION

PLAN - 2

CUBE ELEVATIONS

PLAN - 1

ELEVATION

Specialised drawing packages

Details are drawn to describe their particular conditions, functions or context within a scheme. Certain elements of a scheme (such as a staircase or piece of furniture) may have to be built by manufacturers that are not closely associated with the project. In such cases, a package of bespoke or specialised drawings is compiled. These drawings will contain sufficient information to allow the details to be produced separately and correctly.

Isolating the manufacture of building components in this way allows the scheme design to develop more flexibly and to be informed by a range of different specialists

Full size › **Detail scale** › Interior scale

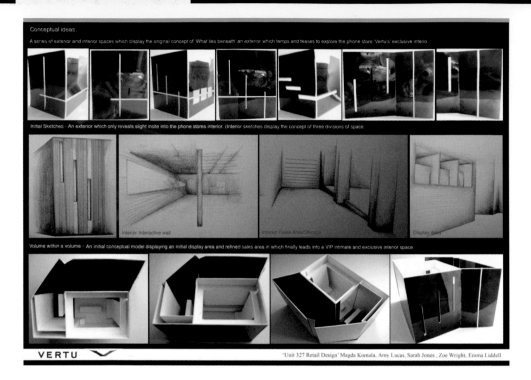

Conceptual ideas:

A series of exterior and interior spaces which display the original concept of 'What lies beneath' an exterior which temps and teases to explore the phone store 'Vertu's' exclusive interio.

Initial Sketches - An exterior which only reveals slight insite into the phone stores interior. (Interior sketches display the concept of three divisions of space)

Interior Interactive wall   Interior Sales Area/Storage   Display Area

Volume within a volume - An initial conceptual model displaying an initial display area and refined sales area in which finally leads into a VIP intimate and exclusive interior space

VERTU

'Unit 327 Retail Design' Magda Kumala, Amy Lucas, Sarah Jones , Zoe Wright, Emma Liddell

Project: Vertu retail store
Location: Conceptual
Designer: Group Project
Date: 2007

This series of images describes the development of an interior design idea for a mobile phone store. The concept started with a series of models that were photographed from the inside to explore the spaces created. Interior sketches then explored the intended views within the store. The final model brings together the contrasting opposites of light and dark, white and black, inside and outside, which were the early concept influences.

When drawing interior spaces, an important consideration is that the whole space needs to be described at once. Doing so allows an understanding between the furniture in the space, the detailed components of the space (such as its light fittings) and the material finish of the space.

Interior space is normally described at 1:10 and 1:20 scale, depending on the size of the room. These drawings are even more effective if they display objects we understand the scale of. For example, if we see a scale drawing of a room with a bed in it, then we can better understand the scale of the room relative to the furniture. This is because a bed is a (largely) uniformly sized object. A scale drawing of a room with a table in it will be less effective as a table can be variable in size.

Placing figures of people in interior drawings also allows the viewer to connect with the scale of the room or the space, and develop an idea of how the space might be utilised.

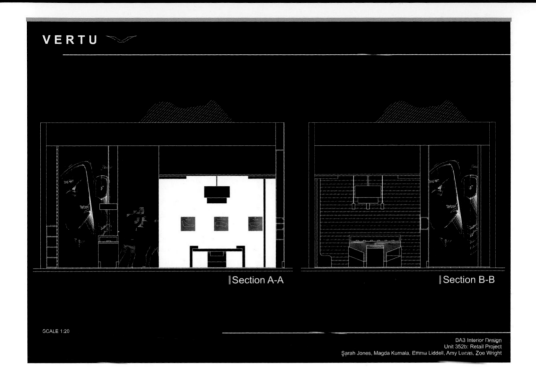

VERTU

| Section A-A | Section B-B

SCALE 1:20

DA3 Interior Design
Unit 352b: Retail Project
Sarah Jones, Magda Kumala, Emma Liddell, Amy Lucas, Zoe Wright

**Project: Vertu retail store
Location: Conceptual
Designer: Group project
Date: 2007**

The Vertu retail store concept was a contrast of space and tone. This section drawing of the phone store incorporates figure that are photomontaged on to the drawing to offer a sense of the store's scale. The positive/negative aspect of the scheme is echoed in the white-on black (reversed) drawing. The focus of the drawings is on the interior space and also the display of the merchandise.

Sample panels

When designing an interior space the use of colour, texture, available light and finish are also key considerations that contribute to an overall scheme. These aspects of design can be varied to produce an array of interior experiences. Much like perspective drawings (see page 52), sample panels or material boards can suggest how the finish of the interior could be executed.

Sample panels can show colour schemes and the finishes of wall coverings and flooring materials and specify particular interior details such as door handles or timber finishes, which may be included to give a real-size example of the intended finish.

Detail scale › **interior scale** › Building scale

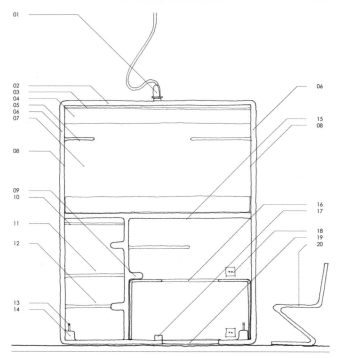

Project: Student housing scheme
Location: Rotterdam,
the Netherlands
Designer: Jeremy Davies
Date: 2007

This proposed housing project used an innovative idea for student accommodation. It comprises a series of large-scale 'trunks' that are self-contained storage, sleeping and study areas. The detail drawing and interior perspective give a good idea of the scale of the design and also how students could inhabit the 'rooms'. The proposal is a unique solution to a common interior space challenge.

Interior and sectional perspective

Interior perspective drawings are a useful way to describe the intended function of a room or space. At interior scale, the sense of interaction that the potential user might have with the space, the atmosphere of it or how they may use it can be communicated.

Often an interior perspective drawing is combined with a section drawing so that the activity that might take place inside the room is conjoined with the sense of how the building is constructed and what the relationships between the interior spaces are. These sectional perspectives connect the viewer with the space more directly by associating the building with a potential experience.

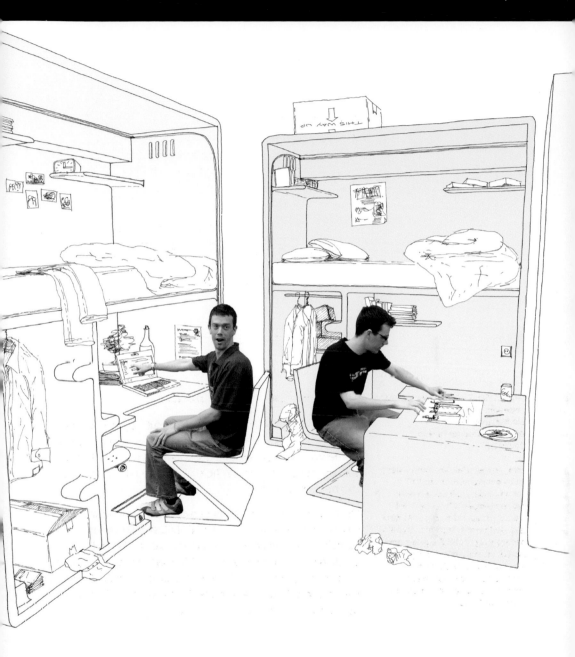

Describing a building accurately will incorporate a variety of scales, but selecting the appropriate scale will depend on the size of the building design. A small house can be drawn at 1:50 scale, which will show (in relative detail) the building and its suggested furniture layout. A larger house or building, however, would be insufficiently described at 1:50 scale and would need to be described at a minimum of 1:100 scale. A larger development, perhaps a development for a block of apartments, would need to be described at a minimum of 1:200 scale – if aspects of landscape and the external surrounding area are important 1:500 may be used (but this scale is relatively diagrammatic).

Building drawings

A set of building drawings should contain enough information so that one can understand all the spatial connections within the scheme as well as the details of its internal layout. It is important to show intended furniture layout in a scheme design as this will help the viewer gain a better understanding of the intended use of the space. The drawings need to collectively describe the whole building as a series of rooms as well as their associated functions.

These building drawings will be further separated into groups to allow different types of information to be described and further developed. For example, a reflected ceiling plan will describe the layout of the lights and other electrical fittings and their location on the building's ceiling. Other layouts might describe furniture configurations, the building's electrical wiring, or its heating and ventilation systems. Each piece of information will be described on a different drawing, to allow clarity and accuracy when designing each of the building's component systems.

Shifting scales

When designing a building the process normally begins with a consideration of site and location, then progresses to the proposal's immediate context. Next, the building layout will need to be developed to ensure that it connects with aspects of route, views and orientation. Finally, detailed consideration is given to the building's materials, components and assembly.

At each stage of design the drawing scale shifts. Location drawings are created at a scale of 1:1250. The next stage of drawings will show more detail, describing form and relationship to site; these drawings will be created at 1:500 scale. Building layout drawings are produced at 1:200 and 1:100 scale to allow the relationships between rooms, spaces, functions and connections to outside spaces to be understood.

All of these drawings can be developed simultaneously and, in some cases, this is preferable as certain drawings (such as plans and sections) need to constantly relate to one another as the building's design is developed, updated and realised.

A great building must begin with the unmeasurable, must go through measurable means when it is being designed and in the end must be unmeasurable.
Louis Kahn

Detail scale › **Building scale** › Urban scale

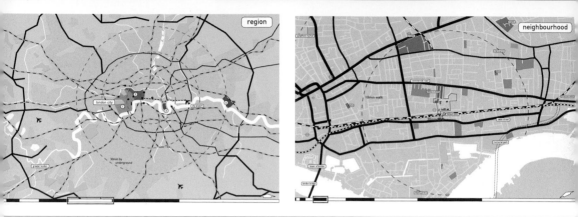

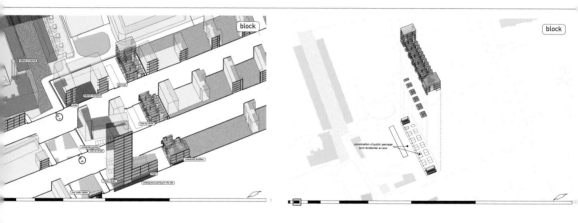

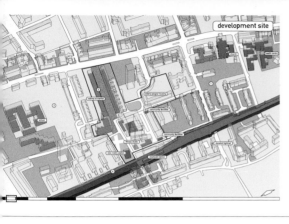

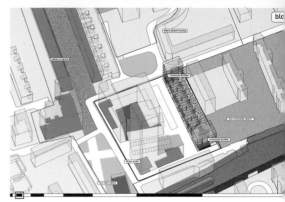

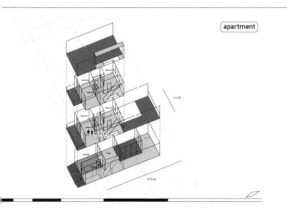

Project: Tarling redevelopment
Location: London, UK
Architect: S333 Architecture
Date: 2005

This series of drawings helps explain the range of scales that are needed to fully communicate an architectural idea. The first drawing is a map (created at urban scale) and then each successive drawing incorporates more detail about the architectural scheme, providing information about the surrounding region, the neighbourhood, the development site, the apartment blocks and finally the individual apartment layout (which is displayed at interior scale). Images from CAD models also help to describe the scheme.

Interior scale › **Building scale** › Urban scale

Google Earth

In 1977, Charles and Ray Eames investigated the concept of scale and presented their results in *The Power of Ten*. This nine-minute film was an investigation into the relative scale of objects and spaces. Starting from a view of two people enjoying a picnic, the film transports the viewer to the outer edges of the known universe. Every ten seconds the picnic spot starting point is seen from ten times farther out, until our own galaxy becomes just a speck of light. The return journey moves inwards at ten times more magnification every ten seconds, until the viewer reaches the hand of one of the picnickers. The journey ends inside a proton of a carbon atom within a DNA molecule in a white blood cell.

The Internet now offers a similar facility via Google's Google Earth software (www.googleearth.com).

Using this software, map coordinates of any place in the world can be discovered and the image of any location can be viewed, showing as much information that has been recorded by the system. In many urban areas this can show great detail, in other places only outlines are shown. This can be used as the basis for a feasibility study for a project in place of any other map.

Cities contain a variety of buildings and spaces (such as parks, schools, shops, apartments or hospitals) that are all united by a network of infrastructures or routes (such as roads and railway lines). To see and understand how all these buildings (or spaces) and routes connect with one another requires the use of scale that cartographers and town planners use: urban (or map) scale. Maps of districts and cities are commonly described using scales of 1:10000, 1:5000 and 1:2500.

When drawing at urban scale, deciding what to include and what to omit is of primary importance. A map is a constructed image and as such should only describe what is necessary within its particular frame of reference.

Using an urban scale in architectural drawing allows a deeper analysis of the site because its location can be described in terms of its relationships with other aspects of the city. Many architectural developments in cities form part of an urban 'strategy', this is a connected design concept that unfolds across a city linking different spaces, buildings and districts.

Some buildings are designed at a vast scale, incorporating parks or promenades or even suggesting new ways of living in the city. To describe these ideas and concepts, a whole section of a city or area needs to be drawn at a map scale of 1:1000 or 1:2500.

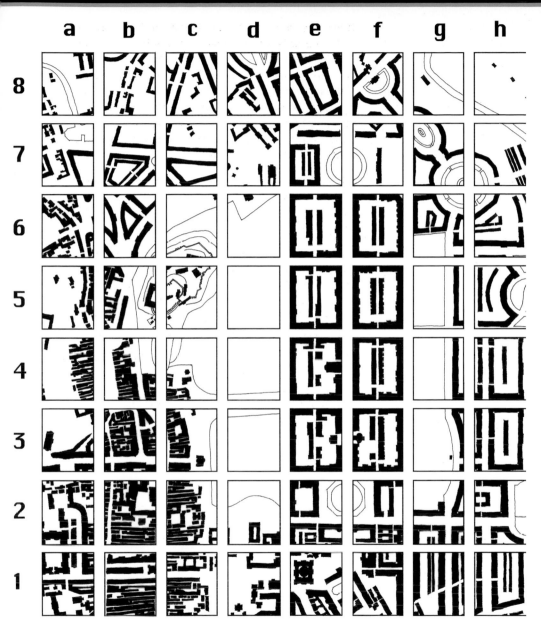

Project: Mapping of Edinburgh
Location: Edinburgh,
Scotland
Architect: David Mathias
Date: 2004

This series of images describe
Edinburgh as a kind of abstract map.
Figure ground mapping technique is
used to describe buildings as solid
blocks and leaves the spaces
between buildings as clear. A grid
reference system is also used to
help locate the individual buildings
on the map.

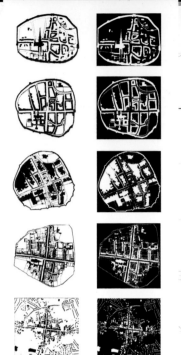

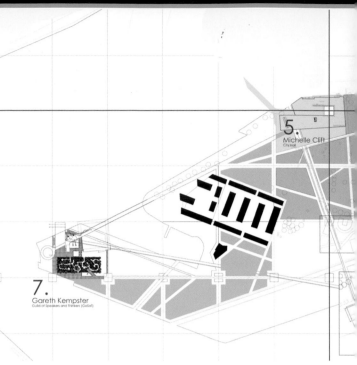

Project: Figure ground urban analysis
Location: Chichester, UK
Designer: Khalid Saleh
Date: 2007

These maps analyse Chichester city centre. The use of black images on a white background and the reverse of white images on a black background creates a contrast and allows an easy understanding of the spaces between the buildings and the density of the buildings in the city plan.

Figure and ground mapping

Giambattista Nolli was a seventeenth-century cartographer who described aspects of space in Rome using a technique called figure and ground mapping. This technique sees buildings displayed as areas of solid blocks and urban spaces are left as clear (or empty) areas. Figure and ground mapping technique is particularly useful when analysing a site to better understand the density of urban spaces.

Maps and mapping

Mapping is a generic term that is used architecturally to describe the relative location of a place or site. But the term can also be applied to the way in which places might be described. A place may be 'mapped' using diagrams, models or drawings.

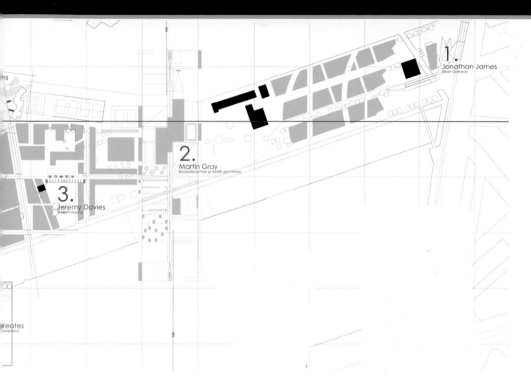

1.
Jonathan James
Urban Gateway

2.
Martin Gray
Recreational Park of Health and Fitness

3.
Jeremy Davies
Student Housing

The location of a site is the starting point for most architecture, so a location map is usually the first descriptive image of most architectural projects. Information such as where the site is, what the site orientation is, or whether or not there any interesting geographical features nearby can be found in a location map, but moreover, location maps can also suggest important considerations for a design (as the scheme could respond to existing buildings and facilities in the area).

Location maps are usually described at the scale of 1:1250 or 1:1000. A scale of 1:500 may also be used to show details of the site's immediate context and surrounding location, particularly in urban areas.

Project: Urban masterplan
Location: Rotterdam, the Netherlands
Designer: The European Studio, University of Portsmouth, UK
Date: 2007

The European Studio developed a masterplan strategy for an 'island' area to the south of Rotterdam. The map shows the overall masterplan idea, which uses a grid to regularise the Island. The map uses figure ground techniques to accentuate areas of space and building form.

Building scale › **Urban scale** › Not to scale

Drawings that are 'not to scale' (NTS) are, as the name suggests, created when scale is unnecessary to explain an idea or concept. If a drawing or model is conceptual, then its scale is irrelevant; what is of primary importance is the form, the idea and the materials. Scale provides a comparative reference, so producing drawings or models that are NTS allows a different sort of consideration; there is a freedom to investigate the architectural design using other parameters. The most often used NTS representational techniques are conceptual designs, experimental models, sketches, photomontages and collages.

Conceptual designs

Particularly appropriate at the initial stages of a project when developing a concept or preliminary design, conceptual drawings allow the architect to move freely through their ideas. The concept can be developed diagrammatically in sketches, or via an investigation of model form, shape or material.

At the conceptual stage of an architectural scheme anything can inform the design development; it may be a process of making or thinking, or a physical sense of form or materiality.

Project: Rough Grounds
Location: Gloucestershire, UK
Architect: Pierre d'Avoine
Architects
Date: 2006

This is one of a group of houses that forms an integral part of a larger rural development for an equestrian centre, which has been conceived as an initiative in agricultural diversification. This perspective drawing shows the house viewed through the trees. The site is part of a Grade I listed landscape on the Westonbirt Estate in Gloucestershire. Octagon House, Belvedere House and the Lodge have been designed together with indoor and outdoor schools and stables, embedded in clearings formed within the woodland plantation known as Rough Grounds. The perspective image shows a veiled view of the building hidden by trees.

'Think simple' as my old master used to say – meaning reduce the whole of its parts into the simplest terms, getting back to first principles.

Frank Lloyd Wright

Experimental modelling

Investigating a proposed architectural design via modelling and sculpting allows the form to be developed through the manipulation of shapes, planes, lines and edges. This design process uses the properties of the modelling material to create architectural form. Scale is not an initial consideration. Experimental modelling is definitely driven by the idea that a building's form follows its function.

Sketching

Most sketches aren't created to scale. These drawings are created for observational, analytical or developmental purposes. This is the advantage of sketching: it allows you to work through a design problem visually and develop your response to it iteratively. Similarly, diagrams used in site or building analysis are not necessarily drawn to scale; often these communicate a specific idea or understanding of a building or space and, as such, scale is again irrelevant.

Photomontage and collage

Photomontage and collage work is not created to any particular scale as the intention underlying these forms of representation is the communication of the architectural idea. These artistic investigations and presentations offer the opportunity to visually explore an idea in a dynamic way and suggest both impossible and possible scenarios and situations.

**Project: Wansey Street social
housing
Location: London, UK
Architect: dRMM
Date: 2005**

The Wansey Street social housing
scheme reinterprets the standard
British terrace house with twenty-first
century requirements for density,
planning flexibility, sustainability,
ownership and security. dRMM's
proposal continues the split-level
arrangement of the adjacent
terraces, with steps and ramps going
down to a garden level approximately
one-metre below the street.

This perspective drawing gives a
glimpse into the courtyard space and
also describes the elevation of the
proposed development and how the
building will connect with the
courtyard design.

Urban scale › **Not to scale** › Exercise 2: scale

This exercise will look at measuring and proportion. You will first measure and draw objects at real size to better understand how the size of these objects alters as they are drawn at a range of different scales. You will draw at:

1:2 scale (half size)
1:20 scale (one-twentieth real size)
1:200 scale (one two-hundredth real size)

Notice that each of these scales increases by a factor of ten.

Sketching to scale
Designer: Nicola Crowson

A useful exercise to better understand scale is to draw an object at full size (or real) scale, and then to draw the object again at different scales. At each stage the rendering of the object will become smaller and smaller and more of the space around it will become evident. This exercise frames the object in different scales.

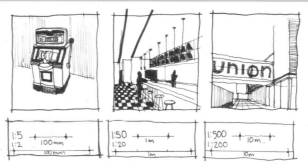

Using appropriate scale

1 Draw a full-page grid in your sketchbook that is composed of 10mm squares.

2 Now find an object to draw and place it on a table. It could be a vase, a cup, a pencil case or anything that is no bigger than a third of your sketchbook page.

3 Using a 3m tape measure, record the dimensions of your object. Now use the grid in your sketchbook to draw a real size (1:1 scale) plan (a horizontal plane through the object), elevation (a side view as viewed from the front, back, left or right) and section (a plane through the object) views of the object.

4 On a fresh sheet draw another full-page grid made of 10mm squares. Each square of this grid will have a different value from the squares in your first grid. The first grid allowed you to record 10mm of the object's information in each square. The value of each square in this new grid will need to incorporate twice as much of the object's information (20mm).

5 Now draw plan, section and elevation views of the object at 1:2 scale. The resultant drawings will now be half the object's real size (1:2).

6 On a fresh sheet draw another full-page grid made of 10mm squares.

7 Now draw a plan, elevation and section view of this object at 1:20 scale. Each square of your grid should now accommodate 200mm. You will have to now draw more information around the object. Details of the table, the room and any other surrounding details will need to be included.

8 On a fresh sheet draw another full-page grid made of 10mm squares.

9 Draw a plan and section of the object at 1:200 scale. Each square is worth 2000mm so the drawings will feature even more of the object's detail, the table and the surrounding space.

Each of these drawings is 10 times smaller than the preceding one. The grid has remained static at 10mm real size, but each drawing becomes relatively smaller, and displays the level or detail and information that is relevant at each scale ratio.

Not to scale › Exercise 2: scale

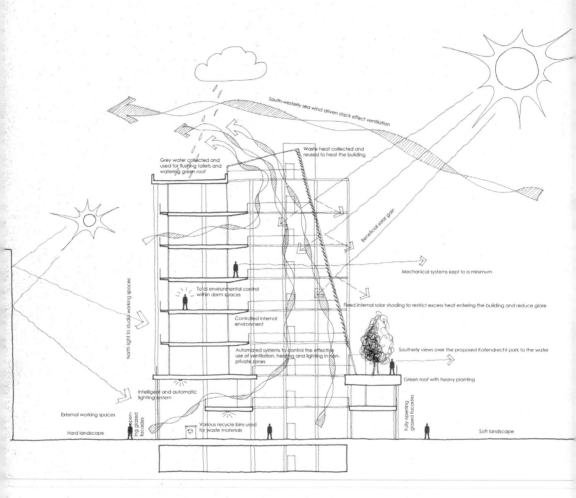

South-westerly sea wind driven stack effect ventilation

Grey water collected and used for flushing toilets and watering green roof

Waste heat collected and reused to heat the building

Beneficial solar gain

North light to study/working spaces

Mechanical systems kept to a minimum

Total environmental control within dorm spaces

Fixed internal solar shading to restrict excess heat entering the building and reduce glare

Controlled internal environment

Southerly views over the proposed Katendrecht park to the water

Automated systems to control the effective use of ventilation, heating and lighting in non-private zones

Green roof with heavy planting

Intelligent and automatic lighting system

External working spaces

Opening glazed facades

Various recycle bins used for waste materials

Fully opening glazed facades

Soft landscape

Hard landscape

Representational techniques

Displaying a proposed piece of architecture as a series of drawings presents an interesting challenge. The information in the drawings needs to be both accurate and interconnected to tell the story of the building and communicate the proposed scheme clearly using a system that is universally recognised and understood. These drawings are two-dimensional images that need to be read and interpreted as a three-dimensional building or space.

Orthographic projection refers to a system of interrelated two-dimensional views of a building. This system includes the views from above or a horizontal cross section of a building (the plan), the views from the side of a building (the elevation) and the views of vertical 'cuts' or cross sections of the building (the section). These drawings can be collectively referred to as a 'full set' and will include all floor plans, the roof plan, all elevations and a series of vertical 'cuts' that explain the internal and external relationships of the building.

Project: Student housing proposal
Location: Rotterdam, the Netherlands
Designer: Jeremy Davies
Date: 2007

This housing scheme proposes a nine-storey block that responds to local (windy) climatic conditions and also exploits its orientation (as a south-facing block) to encourage passive heating through a glazed atrium space.

This section drawing explains all aspects of the scheme. It connects the building to the ground and its context, describes its orientation and the internal connections created via the building's atrium space.

The purpose of these drawings is to technically describe how to physically realise a conceptual idea. The plan is drawn first and section and elevations are then drawn alongside it. Using CAD software, the plans will be carefully drawn on different 'layers' ensuring that the floor plan of the ground and subsequent floors align. This set of drawings then needs to be printed so that the elevations, plans and sections can be seen alongside one another.

Reading plan section and elevation drawings correctly is a skill, and understanding the drawing conventions and the symbols used in them is a necessary part of acquiring this skill. This chapter describes how the convention of plan, section and elevation are used to describe architectural ideas and design buildings and structures.

A plan is an orthographic projection of a three-dimensional object from the position of a horizontal plane through the object. In other words, a plan is a section viewed from above. To plan an architectural idea is to develop and organise its scheme. This is an important and iterative process when designing architecture and the end product of this process is the plan drawing.

Architecture evolves as the plan of a scheme is drawn and redrawn again and again, perhaps shifting elements such as doors and openings, or changing descriptions of the space and its connections with any rooms around it. Creating the plan is the most volatile part of the design process. What starts as a diagram of spaces and shapes with associated functions, becomes more refined as the design evolves.

Planning architecture requires an understanding and appreciation of the relationships between the different spaces within a proposed building or structure. Generating an overview of the whole building is the necessary first step towards this understanding. The overview drawing will be composed as a series of rooms and spaces that are connected by circulation (stairs, lifts or corridors for example).

Once the overview plan has been designed, the building's individual rooms need to be planned in detail by introducing furniture, doors and other elements. As the individual plans of the rooms are worked out, the floor plan is likely to require adjustment as the relationship between the building, its rooms, their functions, and the use of materials, geometry, symmetry and route are further developed.

Project: Chattock House
Location: Newport, Wales
Architect: John Pardey Architects
Date: 2007

The site for this house sits on the northern edge of the Newport Estuary in Pembrokeshire National Park, which is on the westernmost coast of Wales. These plans locate the site of the house and provide information about the immediate context of the site by displaying the surrounding buildings and landscape. The larger plan shows more detail of the landscape around the house and the contours suggest the slope of the site.

Orthographic projection

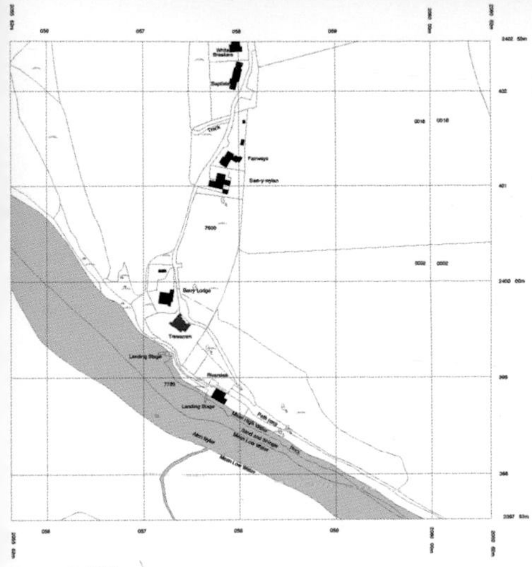

os map @ 1:2500

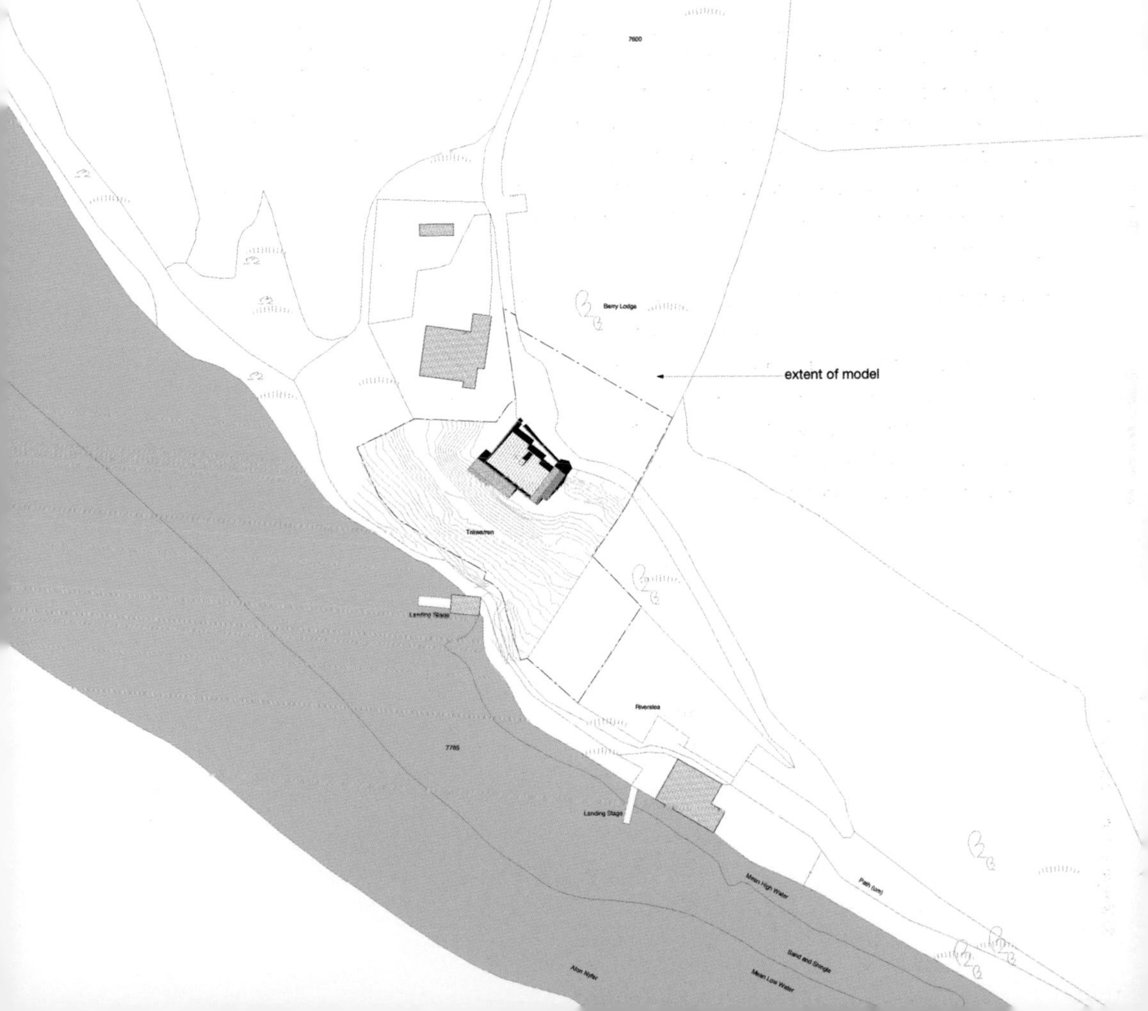
Track
Fairways
Stan-y-wylan
7600
Berry Lodge
extent of model
Trewarren
Landing Stage
Riverslea
7785
Landing Stage
Mean High Water
Path (um)
Sand and Shingle
Afon Nyfer
Mean Low Water

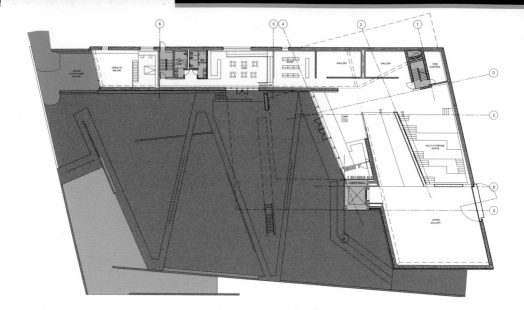

Drawing conventions

When drawing a plan, graphic conventions are used to describe the layout. Incorporating these conventions removes the need to include any accompanying text to further explain the drawing.

Variations in line thickness are used to indicate different degrees of solidity or permanence in the plan. A thicker line suggests more permanence or a denser material (so might be used to signify a masonry wall) and a thinner line suggests a more temporary quality or a lighter material (so might be used to suggest a temporary piece of furniture).

Finally, a plan drawing should always display a north point as this allow an understanding of the proposed building's relationship to its site and orientation and how sunlight will affect its different spaces.

Drawing conventions should be acknowledged, and plan drawings need to be consistent in their use of them. However, some architects may adopt a more idiosyncratic approach to their application of symbols and the types of information included in their drawings, which will create a distinctive, if not universal, practice style.

Orthographic projection

**Project: Nanjing Museum of Art
and Architecture
Location: Nanjing, China
Architect: Steven Holl Architects
Date: 2006**

This new museum, sited near
Nanjing, China, is formed by a
'field' of parallel perspective spaces
and garden walls (as shown in the
site plan above). The museum's
upper gallery, suspended high in
the air, unwraps in a clockwise
turning sequence and culminates at
'in-position' viewing of the city of
Nanjing in the distance.

Shown on the facing page is the
museum's ground plan.

Types of plan

An architectural scheme will require a range of plan 'types'
to be created. A ground plan is a horizontal cut through a
building (it cuts through the building's walls, windows and
openings) drawn at approximately 1200m above the floor
plane. A ground plan reveals the connections between inside
and outside spaces, between internal rooms and layouts and
between the materials from which the building is made.

The ground floor plan should show the entrance to the
building and its relationship to the exterior spaces and
gardens. Other level floor plans, such as first or second
floor plans, will clearly indicate staircases and connections
between the building's levels. In cases where the floor plan
is repetitive, for example in a housing or office block, then
only one indicative plan may be shown to suggest the
general layout of the building.

The roof plan should indicate the slope of the roof and its
overhang on the walls. It may be shown separately or it may
be incorporated in the site plan.

A location plan will be used to display the building within
the context of its site or surroundings. It should clearly
describe the proposed building's location in relationship to
any surrounding important geographical or physical features
such as local roads or important civic buildings.

A site plan will present a description of the building in the
context of its site, and include surrounding buildings and
other significant routes, paths, trees or surrounding planting.
A site plan shows these elements in more detail than a
location plan. The site plan may be combined with the
ground plan.

Aligning plans

It is crucial that all types of plans for a particular building or scheme align with one another. When creating freehand plans and developing your scheme it is useful to draw each one on tracing paper as these can be laid over one another to ensure that they all align.

In CAD software, the floor plans are drawn on top of one another to ensure that they fully align. There are also facilities within CAD programmes to repeat floor plans and to read them simultaneously. Essentially the drawings exist as a series of 'layers' within the program and each floor plan will be drawn on a different layer. This allows plans to be reproduced and altered quickly.

It is also important to ensure that floor plans are all aligned with the north point (or as near as possible to it), and all floor plans should be presented in the same orientation on a sheet to avoid any confusion when they are read together.

Project: School of Art and Art History, University of Iowa
Location: Iowa, USA
Architect: Steven Holl Architects
Date: 2006

The University of Iowa's new School of Art and Art History is a hybrid structure of open edges and an open centre. Instead of an object, the building is a 'formless' instrument. Flat or curved planes are slotted together or assembled with hinged sections. Flexible spaces open out from studios in warm weather, and the main horizontal passages are meeting places with interior glass walls that reveal work-in-progress.

This series of plans show the relationship of the different floor plans and also the relationship to the site and the surrounding landscape.

Orthographic projection

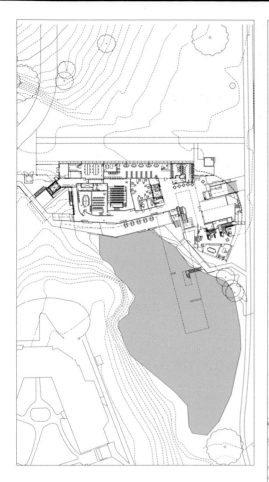

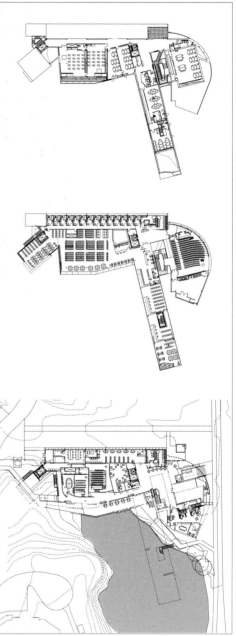

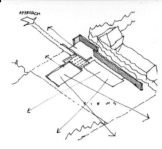

Project: Duckett House
Location: New Forest, UK
Architect: John Pardey Architects
Date: 2005

This range of drawings shows a concept perspective sketch (above) that explains the relationship of the building elements, a site plan (right) and more detailed layout plans of ground and first floors (facing page).

Set within a conservation area, this private house aims to achieve a contemporary outlook that remains in-keeping with its sensitive context. The concept is based on the idea of creating an architecture that respects the idea of vernacular buildings by avoiding a single form in favour of an assemblage of smaller elements. The house therefore divides into three functions; guest/study, living and sleeping. These are used to create three interlocking forms that are clad in cedar above a white wall. A central chimney anchors the composition and rises above a black zinc roof that echoes traditional slate.

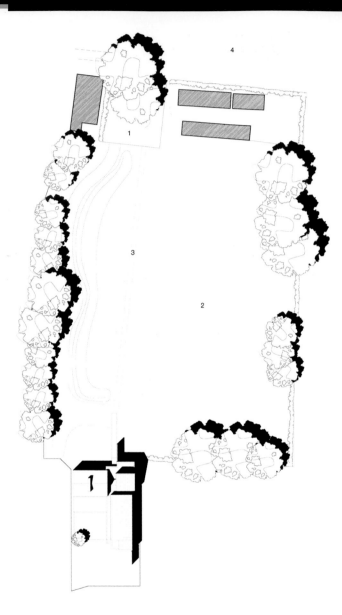

Orthographic projection

A section drawing is an orthographic projection of a three-dimensional object from the position of a vertical plane through the object. In other words, it is a vertical cut through a building. A section drawing is one of the most useful and revealing drawings in the design and description of a building. As with all two-dimensional drawings, a section is an abstract representation. It would be impractical and impossible to actually slice through a building and reveal its internal connections, so a useful analogy is to consider cutting through something it is possible to slice. For example, if you cut a piece of fruit, such as an apple, it will become immediately apparent that its skin is very thin and its flesh is relatively solid and dense, but if you slice an orange you will expose a thicker skin protecting a softer fruit inside.

Section drawings communicate the connection between the inside and the outside of a building and the relationships between the building's rooms. They can also display the thickness of the building's walls and their relationship to internal elements such as the roof, the external boundary walls, gardens and other spaces.

Without accompanying section drawings, the building plans can only suggest spatial arrangements. Once the section drawings are read alongside the plans, the heights of ceilings, doors and windows, double height spaces or mezzanine decks can be described and explained. Together, the section and plan drawings allow the three-dimensional picture of the building to be better understood.

Project: Nanjing Museum of Art and Architecture
(facing page, top)
Location: Nanjing, China
Architect: Stephen Holl Architects
Date: 2006

This section drawing shows the relationship between the museum and its landscape. Part of the scheme is set within the landscape, and the upper gallery is supported above the lower part of the building allowing views across the surrounding area.

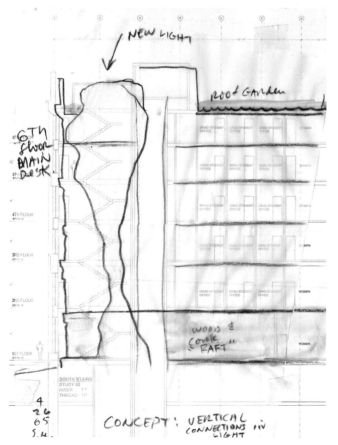

Project: New York University
Location: New York City, USA
Architect: Steven Holl Architects
Date: 2007

This concept section drawing was
produced as part of a design scheme
for the interior renovation of an 1890
corner building at the New York
University. The concept organises
new spaces around light and the
phenomenal properties of materials.
A new stair shaft below a new
skylight joins the six-level building
vertically with a shifting porosity
of light and shadow that change
seasonally. The ground level, utilised
by the entire university, contains a
new curvilinear wooden auditorium
on a cork floor.

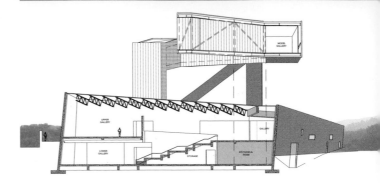

**Project: Nanjing Museum
of Art and Architecture
Location: Nanjing, China
Architect: Steven Holl Architects
Date: 2006**

This long section drawing describes
the relationship between the various
galleries on the museum's lower
block and the storage and plant
hidden underneath. There is another
building element raised above that
houses a model gallery.

Long and short sections

As with architectural plans, simply producing a single section
drawing of a proposed building is insufficient. The different
section drawings should be taken from the most interesting,
complex or unusual parts of the plan and will explain an
aspect of the building that cannot be understood from the
plan drawings alone. A long section drawing is created from
the longest part of the plan to show the interrelationships
between the areas within it. A short section drawing is taken
from the narrowest part of the plan.

All section drawings are individually labelled (the standard
convention is to use AA, BB, CC and so on for each one) and
the corresponding labels are displayed on the plan to show
where the section line is cut. Section drawings are also
labelled with their orientation points (north, east, etc.) so that
they can be read in conjunction with the elevation drawings.

Sections and other representations

Other forms of representation can be combined with section drawings to create useful interpretations of a building. For example, a sectional perspective drawing combines a two-dimensional section drawing with a three-dimensional perspective drawing. This can create a powerful image that suggests how the internal spaces within the building can be used.

Physical models that are built in the form of a sectional cut can also allow the inside of a proposed building to be better understood. Creating a series of sectional models can fully explain a complex scheme and its relationship to the surrounding landscape or environment. Hinged sectional models can be opened and closed to reveal the internal spaces in a building.

Project: Chattock House
Location: Newport, UK
Architect: John Pardey Architects
Date: 2007

These long and short section drawings are taken through the plan drawings of the scheme and relate the architecture to the landscape and immediate surroundings. The section drawings need to be read in conjunction with the plan.

Project: Nanjing Museum
of Art and Architecture (right)
Location: Nanjing, China
Architect: Steven Holl Architects
Date: 2004

Models are very effective means of exploring the sectional idea of a building. They can be photographed to create a series of views (shown here is a perspective view into the space and a long sectional view). This sectional model describes how light enters into the building and the connections between various floor levels of the interior spaces.

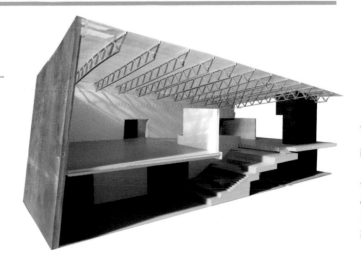

Plans › **Sections** › Elevations

white render
cedar cladding panels
timber sliding screens
powder coated aluminium windows
colured render
glazed balustrade
standing seam zinc roof
rendered chimney
garage set within hillside

Project: Chattock House
Location: Newport, Wales
Architect: John Pardey Architects
Date: 2007

This drawing describes the west elevation of the scheme and also provides heights to relate the building to its landscape levels. Figures in the drawing allow the relative scale of the building to be understood and the shading suggests shadow from overhanging elements of the roof.

In architectural terms, an elevation drawing describes the vertical plane of a building or space. An elevation drawing can be an external view (for example, of a building or street), or an internal one (for example, of a room).

The elevation is the interface between the inside and the outside of a building. Buildings can be designed from the outside to the inside by using the elevation to generate the internal plan. However, most architects usually begin the design process with the plan, and the elevation drawings are created in response to it. This means that elevation drawings are often drawn and redrawn as the plan evolves so that design decisions can be understood and connected to the external form.

Elevation drawings are normally labelled with the direction that the elevation faces, (so the south elevation is south facing, the north elevation is north facing and so on). This connects the elevations directly to the orientation of the plan, and immediately allows an understanding of how the sunlight will affect the building over the course of the day and with the change of the seasons.

Orthographic projection

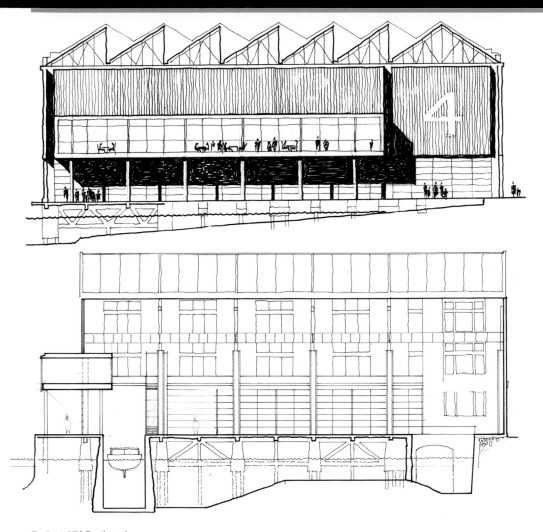

Project: HM Dockyard
Location: Portsmouth, UK
Architects: Colin Stansfield Smith
and John Pardey Architects
Date: 2005

These are elevation drawings
of an existing building and proposed
scheme. Shown at the top is the
south-east elevation drawing
and beneath is the internal
elevation drawing.

Both images are carefully hand
drawn and considered, using a
variety of line weights to describe
the different aspects of the
architecture. There is a clear line
hierarchy in each drawing.

Sections › **Elevations** › Drawing conventions

Elevation and context

The most important aspect of an elevation is that it forms the 'skin' of the building. As such a building's elevations need to relate to their context or surrounding environment. This requires the architect to develop a solid understanding of any surrounding buildings and aspects of the existing architecture (such as the materials they use, or their scale, massing and height), and the rhythm of a proposed location. All this will provide clues for an appropriate architectural response and suggest how a proposed design might respond to its context. Drawings of any proposed buildings should incorporate the elevation views of the surrounding architecture so that the scale of the proposed building can be understood.

Context doesn't need to be thought of as a limiting factor. In fact it helps to locate the architecture. However, the choice or precedent of scale, mass or materials used will affect aspects of the elevation. For example, if the windows are pushed back within the building's elevation, there will be a greater sense of shadow around the window openings. Such features can all be explored in elevation drawings and in doing so help the architect consider different possibilities and variations before deciding which approach or solution is most appropriate.

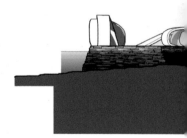

A well-designed elevation will respond to and complement its location and context in terms of use of materials, massing and scale. As a piece of design it needs to be balanced and well proportioned, but equally, it will also need to respond to the requirements of the building layout, with appropriate openings for views and access. The elevation needs to mediate between these two challenging aspects of architectural design.

South Elevation 1:100

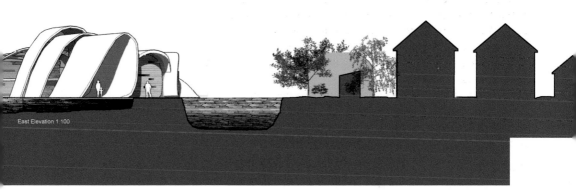

East Elevation 1:100

Project: Emsworth Activity Centre
Location: Emsworth, UK
Designer: Rocky Marchant
Date: 2007

This schematic design has engaged with the challenges that a sculptural form presents. The design idea responded to the site context and this is typified by the form's organic shape, which is inspired by the sea. This form determined the choice of material used and the structural system within the building. The design evolved from a series of physical models that first established form and then the building's functions were introduced as the form was modified and developed.

These elevations show the site and its surroundings, sea to one side, suburban housing to the other.

Sections › **Elevations** › Drawing conventions

Architectural drawings use a distinct 'language' of convention systems that are used universally to enable the information they contain to be easily understood with little or no need for additional explanatory text.

Scale

One of the most useful conventions is the incorporation of scale. Ideally, the title of an architectural drawing should describe the scale used, but if not a measuring rule can be drawn at the side of the drawing as a reference. Information about a drawing's scale provides the viewer with a better understanding of the scheme's proportions and helps to communicate the proposal's information clearly.

Orientation

A north point that indicates the orientation of the building is an essential aspect of a site or ground plan. The direction and flow of natural light into a space and how it is modified, are important considerations for architects. Understanding the building's orientation will also explain many aspects of the internal layout and spatial organisation shown in the plan.

Line thickness

In architectural drawings the thickness of the drawn line has a meaning that communicates a design intention. The general rule in an architectural drawing is that the thicker the line the denser the material, or the more permanent the object being described. Thinner lines are used for furniture and variable elements in the plan, and are often used to communicate additional information about the scheme. Thick lines will be more legible and read as a primary layer of information, whilst the thinner lines read as a secondary layer.

If creating a section drawing, the standard convention is to make the lines thicker at the point where the building has been 'cut'. This distinction allows the viewer to identify where the cut has been made in relation to the plan (the corresponding plan drawing has lines that will indicate where the section drawing has been taken).

Orthographic projection

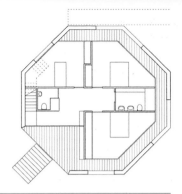

Project: Drum House
Location: Conceptual
Architect: Pierre d'Avoine
Architects
Date: 2005

The Drum House is a prototype model of vertical living, which continues the genre of octagon houses established in the mid-nineteenth century. It was argued then that the advantage of the octagon form was that it could provide more sunlight, ventilation, and good views from every room, and made more efficient use of internal space.

In this prototype, the house is elevated above ground level, and has an inner and outer envelope, with a circulation stair attached to the outer envelope. The freestanding, self-contained structure can be rotated to suit any orientation, making it highly adaptable.

The plan shows the elevated ground floor, containing children's bedrooms or a separate flat. Other floors include the first floor, containing a double-height living space, second floor, with study and winter garden, third floor, containing the master bedroom suite opening onto a deck, and roof levels.

Staircases

Staircases exist between two or more floor levels, and they need to be communicated on a plan drawing. The standard convention is that the staircase is drawn as a solid line up to 1200mm above floor level, and as a dotted line above this level. An arrow is used to indicate the direction of movement up a staircase.

Materials

Materials and their intended use in a building are also communicated in architectural drawings, specifically the plan drawing, which will explain layout and spatial organisation. Different materials are denoted by variations in shading and hatching conventions.

Symbols

Symbols are frequently used in architectural drawings as a form of shorthand to describe the position and location of elements in the building. This shorthand is used by all members of the construction team from building contractors, suppliers and installers to architects and designers.

When creating a freehand line drawing these symbols can be generated using a template. If creating digital drawings, CAD software programmes incorporate object libraries, allowing the user to select the relevant symbol and position it on their drawing. Recognised symbols include pieces of furniture (which give scale to the drawings and can indicate suggested internal layout), bathroom fittings (such as a bath, shower or sink) and kitchen fittings (to show the location of the sink or cooker).

Electrical and mechanical layout drawings have to explain an invisible network of cables, ducts and switches. These drawings also need to incorporate standard conventions and relate to the practical functional requirements of the building. Dotted lines are used to explain runs of cables and connections in the building. Light switches and electrical switches have their own coding system. All these code and symbol systems will be described and explained on the drawing in a legend.

There are various stages in the development of the architectural design that have different categories of drawings associated with them.

Feasibility study drawings

The first of these stages is a feasibility study; this is a preliminary study undertaken to determine and document a project's viability. The results of this study are used to determine whether or not to proceed with the project. At this stage the site, plan drawings, elevations and relevant section drawings will all be required. As the scheme develops, the range of drawings necessary to fulfill the different information requirements increases. For example, further sets of drawings will be produced to request permission to build, or for public consultation exercises.

Presentation drawings

Presentation drawings are normally intended for a client audience. As such they need to be persuasive as they must present the strongest and most convincing aspects of the scheme design. These drawings need to have impact, be accessible, easy to understand and communicate the scheme concepts clearly.

At the stage of public consultation or planning, a set of presentation drawings is needed to explain the relationship of the scheme to its immediate context and the impact the building may have on its site.

Working drawings

Further stages of the design's development will have more detailed sets of drawings associated with them. The drawings that are used to build a piece of architecture is described as a 'working set'. These will include plans, sections and elevations, as well as detailed drawings and sections that explain room layout and specifications that describe materials and other aspects of construction.

The details within this range of drawings will provide information about the structure of the building and elements of its construction, such as the relationship between the walls and the foundation, the walls and the internal floors and the walls and the roof. Any project-specific or specialised details will also be included; these may be bespoke aspects of the architecture that need to be built in a specific way, or an unusual or innovative use of a particular building material.

Coordinated production information (CPI) is an acknowledged scale system that is applied to working drawings. Different drawing types will be created in different scale ratios. For example, exterior information is produced at 1:100 or 1:50 scale (depending on the size of the building), interior information will be provided at 1:50 or 1:20 scale, and the detailed drawings will be provided at 1:5, 1:10 and 1:2 scale.

Working drawings are issued at the point when the scheme is agreed. But on site, as problems or issues crop up, revisions to the drawings may be made. Availability of materials, changes in programming, or an alteration in the client's requirements may mean that alterations are necessary. If, however, one drawing is revised, then all other drawings that relate to it must also be amended in order to ensure that the drawings still work in conjunction with one another to provide a 'full set' of information.

Specialised drawings

Specialised drawings allow the manufacture of particular, perhaps bespoke, items by a supplier. Structural, mechanical and environmental engineers will also issue specialised drawings that respond to specific design problems or issues.

1

AA
03

s.o.p. + 5.375

250 x 125 mm parallam eaves beam

22 mm western red cedar onto
25 x 50 mm battens laid diagonally
@ 400 c-c's onto building paper to
18 mm wbp ply on 125 mm studs @
400 c-c's with infill rigid insulation

50

2425

anthracite zinc standing seam roofing
18 mm wbp ply
241 mm TJI rafters at 400 c-c's
175 mm mineral wool insulation
15 mm pasterboard + skim
125 mm tibeer joists with
jablite insulation
vertical cedar boarding
vertical cedar boarding
single ply membrane on
ply decking

recess

AA
08/09

single ply membrane
18 mm wbp ply on firing pieces to 1:60 fall
expanded urethane insulation
vapour check
plaster board with skim coat

AA
08

t/o joist +2.900

u/s joist +2.700

anthracite zinc
coping

t/o joist +2.850
u/s joist +2.700

150

15

AA
02

250 x 125 mm parallam beam

250 mm deep nisch for sculpture

nom. 25 mm sand/ cement render

75 mm block work

75 mm cavity with
75 mm urethane insulation

100 mm internal leaf block

15 mm plaster

concrete plinth/ hearth

W 2

s.o.p for roof
+ 2.425

50

2425

2700

W 3

2135

2185

1150

nom. 25 mm sand/
cement render

150 mm stud work

150 mm urethane
insulation

FFL +0.125

SSL +0.000

blue/ black semi
engineering brick

FFL +0.125

SSL +0.000

blue/ black semi engineering
brick in black mortar

125

AA
01

Orthographic projection

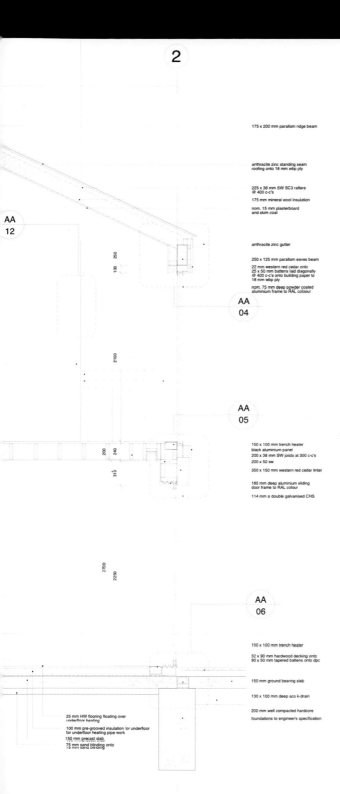

2

175 x 200 mm parallam ridge beam

anthracite zinc standing seam
roofing onto 18 mm wbp ply

225 x 38 mm SW SC3 rafters
@ 400 c-c's
175 mm mineral wool insulation
nom. 15 mm plasterboard
and skim coat

AA
12

anthracite zinc gutter

250 x 125 mm parallam eaves beam
22 mm western red cedar onto
25 x 50 mm battens laid diagonally
@ 400 c-c's onto building paper to
18 mm wbp ply
nom. 75 mm deep powder coated
aluminium frame to RAL colour

AA
04

AA
05

150 x 100 mm trench heater
black aluminium panel
200 x 38 mm SW joists at 300 c-c's
200 x 50 sw

350 x 150 mm western red cedar lintel

185 mm deep aluminium sliding
door frame to RAL colour

114 mm ø double galvanised CHS

AA
06

150 x 100 mm trench heater

32 x 90 mm hardwood decking onto
90 x 50 mm tapered battens onto dpc

150 mm ground bearing slab

130 x 100 mm deep aco k-drain

200 mm well compacted hardcore

foundations to engineer's specification

25 mm HW flooring floating over
underfloor heating
100 mm pre-grooved insulation for underfloor
for underfloor heating pipe work
150 mm precast slab
75 mm sand blinding onto
75 mm sand blinding

Project: Duckett House
Location: New Forest, UK
Architect: John Pardey Architects
Date: 2005

Every design project will require
a set of detailed drawings that
explain the building's assembly and
construction. This set of drawings
forms part of a package of
information designed to assist
in the construction of the building.
The package will include detailed
information about size and
dimension of fixtures, fittings and
any specialised components
needed. All aspects of each
designed component need to be
communicated from, for example,
the material specification for a
staircase to the size of its
accompanying handrail. This
detailed section drawing of Duckett
House explains the building's
materiality providing information as
detailed aspects of construction.

Drawing conventions › Drawing categories › Exercise 3: drawing

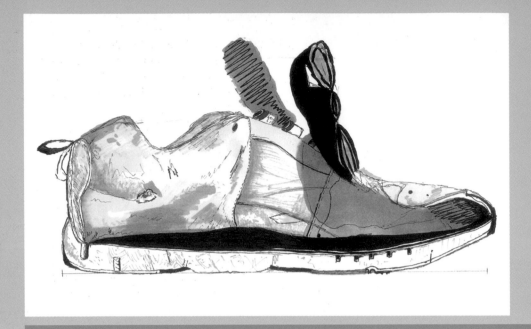

A set of drawings that describes a building or space will contain a range of plans, sections and, elevations. Drawing a section is to imagine a vertical cut through a building. This is an abstract idea and, when first creating a section drawing, it can help to take an object and literally cut or slice it in half (vertically). This process will reveal the relationship between the exterior of an object and its internal qualities. Once this abstract idea takes a real form, the idea of the section through a room, building or landscape can be better understood.

The sectional cut

This exercise is intended to explain and explore the sectional cut and drawing. Sometimes it is difficult to understand what the section of an object or building describes, but essentially it reveals the hidden aspects of a structure.

1 Find an old shoe and saw it in half along its length. Be careful when cutting as some shoes have hidden steel plates.

2 Look at the cut carefully to try and begin to understand its form and how it appears to be assembled. Is it layered? What are the different materials it is made from?

3 Take the shoe and position it so that it is ready to draw (consider the light or shadow falling on it and its surrounding context). Now look again, what surface is it sat on? What is inside? What do you see beyond?

4 Once you have looked at the shoe in great detail, you will be able to make an informed decision about the medium and paper you wish to use. The medium and paper chosen should bear relation to your chosen drawing technique. For example, an ink drawing on cartridge paper will be more precise than an ink drawing on watercolour paper due to its absorbency.

5 Draw only what you see, but draw in detail and at full scale (1:1).

Shoe section

Once drawn, the section allows an understanding of the inside of the shoe and how this relates to the outside form. Sometimes the external shape may suggest something that differs from the internal space. It also reveals the materiality of the shoe, the thickness of the material, its layers of construction and structure.

It can sometimes be difficult to read two-dimensional architectural drawings because certain drawing conventions can appear like a specialised code. Two-dimensional architectural drawings are often attempting to represent three-dimensional spaces or places, which is not always easy. Three-dimensional images can make the interpretation of a building so much easier, and create an impression of a building that is immediately accessible.

Each of the different three-dimensional drawing techniques explored in this chapter can provide a different way to view the building. Perspective drawings allow the view from a particular standpoint, and axonometric and isometric drawings create three-dimensional forms from a particular point, which can be viewed in the same way as a model. The choice of view is the most important consideration when deciding which image type is relevant

Three-dimensional images create an impression of what it might be like to occupy or work in a building, and can be combined with other two-dimensional drawings to give a convincing overall impression of a scheme or project.

Project: Kolata Living Steel Competition
Location: Kolata, India
Architect: Piercy Conner Architects
Date: 2006

Piercy Conner Architects recognise that contemporary housing rarely deviates from the accepted model of sealed cellular spaces, which often fails to respond to demographic and environmental conditions. So in designing for an Indian location, their challenge was to create an economically viable alternative that would be 'expressive, joyful and responsive to the environment'.

This CAD image presents a perspective model of the scheme. The bird's eye view is taken from second-floor level and it allows an understanding of the relationship between the buildings and the street, and also gives a glimpse of the rooftop gardens. Shadow and texture give a sense of reality to the image.

**Project: Nelson-Atkins Museum
of Art
Location: Kansas City, USA
Architect: Steven Holl Architects
Date: 2006**

This competition-winning addition
to the Nelson Atkins Museum of Art
is composed of five interconnected
structures. Traversing from the
existing building across a sculpture
park, the five built 'lenses' form new
spaces and angles of vision creating
new experiences of the existing
museum. This interior sketch
explores the quality of light inside
the gallery space.

**Although perspective images usually offer a true
impression of a space, there are distortions in
perspective that can make the impossible appear
possible.**

There is a sense that perspective images project a true and
measured reality, but they are in fact open to interpretation
and manipulation by the architect or artist, who will decide
what is and isn't seen and where the perspective's viewpoint
is taken from.

Standpoint

All perspectives images are taken from a particular view or
standpoint. The standpoint will determine everything about
the view that is described. It is usually taken at a standard
eye-level height, but it can be manipulated so that the view
is altered. A bird's-eye view, for example, is a standpoint from
above, producing a perspective that reads as if one is flying
over the scheme. A worm's-eye view produces a contrasting
perspective, looking at the scheme from underneath.

action room / classroom

exhibition

individual action centre

reception / security

shop

The picture plane

A picture plane is the imaginary flat surface located between the viewer's standpoint and the object being viewed. Ordinarily, it is a vertical plane that is perpendicular to the horizontal projection of the line of sight to the object's point of interest. The nearer the picture plane is to the object, the larger the image will be. If the picture plane is further away, the resulting image will be smaller.

The picture plane is a concept borrowed from fine art. Albrecht Dürer (1471–1528) developed a grid through which a three-dimensional scene could be depicted with accuracy on a flat plane.

By positioning the grid close to the subject matter, drawing a similar grid pattern onto the paper and using the lines on the grid and the corresponding lines on the paper as a sort of 'map', the artist could transfer what they saw onto the paper surface. Using the grid helped ensure that all aspects of the subject remained in proportion.

Project: Amnesty International head offices
Location: London, UK
Architect: Witherford Watson Mann
Date: 2003

This is a single-point perspective drawing of a proposed entrance to Amnesty International's Human Rights Action Centre in London. The drawing shows the visual relationships between the street, exhibition and campaigns offices and the education rooms. The drawing deliberately foregrounds Amnesty's self-representations, leaving the architecture as the frame for a set of relationships and activities.

Perspective › Axonometric drawings

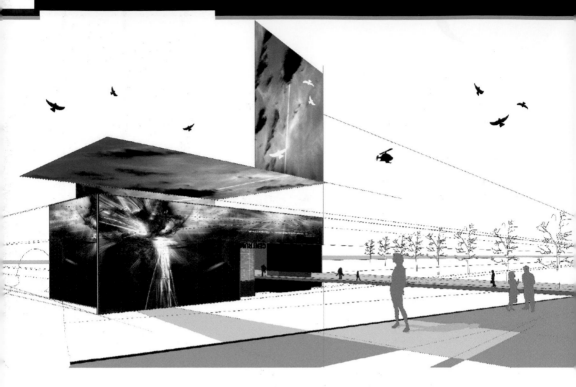

**Project: Rotterdam Photography
Museum
Location: Rotterdam,
the Netherlands
Designer: David Yeates
Date: 2007**

This scheme used the museum's
subject matter, photography, as its
concept generator. The building was
a projection screen to the outside
space. This CAD perspective is
generated from CAD software.

The vanishing point

Perspective views can be single-, two-, or three-point
representations. These points correspond to the number of
points at which all lines in the drawing appear to converge.
Each point of convergence is called the vanishing point.

A single-point perspective drawing has a central vanishing
point, which will exaggerate the sense of a space's depth.
Single-point perspective is often used for interior drawings.
Two-point perspective images are often used to describe
smaller buildings in a space or street context. Three-point
perspective images are used to describe larger buildings
and their surrounding environment and context.

The horizon

The eye-level line in a perspective drawing is referred to as the horizon. The point of horizon is normally about 1.6 metres above floor level, but this can be altered to obtain different viewpoints (such as a worm's- or a bird's- eye view).

Sketch perspective

To sketch in perspective is to first observe and study a view, and then draw to achieve an image that accurately renders that view. This requires some consideration of the vanishing point and of the horizon. Sketch perspective is a useful tool to quickly communicate a realistic impression of an existing space or to suggest a design concept.

Constructed perspective

A constructed perspective is a freehand drawing created from plan, section and elevation information. To create a constructed perspective it is first necessary to decide the standpoint of the drawing and to then use the section and elevation drawings to suggest the details of heights of spaces and openings such as doors and windows. There are important principles when creating a perspective image; these are:

- all lines must converge into the vanishing point,

- figures should get smaller as they move towards the centre of the image and towards the vanishing point,

- space and depth must be maintained in the image to reinforce the illusion of the perspective and its suggested reality.

Project: Student housing scheme
Location: Rotterdam,
the Netherlands
Designer: Jeremy Davies
Date: 2007

This sketch perspective drawing effectively uses colour to animate the building's elevation. Scaled figures are also used to give a sense of reality and activity to the space around the building.

Project: Saïd Business School,
Oxford University
Location: Oxford, UK
Architects: Dixon Jones
Date: 2005

This worm's eye view axonometric drawing presents an unusual abstract perspective of a proposal for a courtyard space in the Saïd Business School. The image allows the scale of the space to be quickly understood.

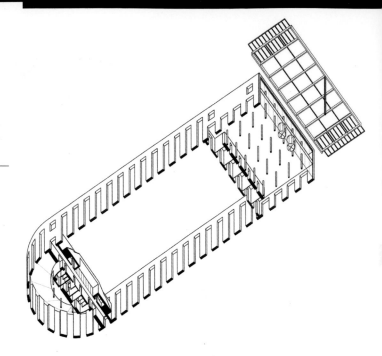

An axonometric drawing (which is also known as a plan oblique drawing) is produced from a plan drawing and is the easiest of the three-dimensional projections to draw. Axonometric drawings allow an overall aerial view of an object. The advantage an axonometric drawing provides to the architect is that it allows an understanding of both the plan and the building's internal or external elevations.

Architectural historian Auguste Choisy (1841–1909) first used axonometric drawings in the nineteenth century and they have been employed by numerous influential twentieth-century artists and architects ever since, including the Russian Constructivists, Kasemir Malevich (1878–1935), El Lissitzky (1890–1941) and Gerrit Rietveld (1888–1964). For these artists and architects axonometric drawings connected very well with their avant-garde architectural and artistic style. For example, the axonometric technique complemented the De Stijl movement's cubist forms of architecture. Today architects such as Zaha Hadid continue to favour axonometric techniques as a signature style of expression.

Project: Phare Tower
Location: Paris, France
Architects: Morphosis
Date: 2006

The Phare Tower scheme in Paris comprises not only of the tower element, but also a lower building that connects with the surrounding urban space. This diagram explains the connections between these building elements and how they relate to the streetscape.

Perspective › **Axonometric drawings** › Isometric drawings

Art and architecture

Constructivism

Constructivism was an artistic and architectural movement in Russia from 1919 onward that dismissed 'pure' art in favour of an art that was used as an instrument for social purposes, specifically the construction of a socialist system.

De Stijl

De Stijl, from the Dutch term for 'the style', was a Dutch artistic movement founded in 1917. De Stijl was also the name of a journal that was published by the painter and critic Theo van Doesburg. Next to Van Doesburg, the group's principal members were the painters Piet Mondrian and Bart van der Leck, and the architects Gerrit Rietveld and JJP Oud.

Proponents of De Stijl sought to express a new utopian ideal of spiritual harmony and order. They advocated pure abstraction and universality by a reduction to the essentials of form and colour — they simplified visual compositions to the vertical and horizontal directions, and used only primary colours along with black and white.

Avant-garde

'Avant-garde' in French means front guard, advance guard, or vanguard and the term is often used to refer to people or works that are experimental or novel, particularly with respect to art, culture and architecture. Avant-garde represents a pushing of the boundaries of what is accepted as the norm, or the status quo, primarily in the cultural realm.

Producing an axonometric drawing

To produce an axonometric drawing you need to redraw or recreate a plan view at an angle of 45 degrees to the horizontal. The plan needs to be orientated so that the right view is achieved axonometrically, for example, there may be a particular elevation aspect of the building that needs to be represented. At this new orientation, the plan is redrawn and all lines are projected vertically. All measures remain 'real' and are taken from the elevation and section drawings.

Once the overall form or framework of the axonometric drawing is achieved, it is then possible to 'cut away' sections to reveal details of the building's interior or its construction. Axonometric drawings allow a simultaneous view of the inside and outside of a building.

Exploded axonometric drawings

Exploded axonometric drawings can explain a concept or idea as a series of visual components. This drawing type is useful to explain a complex idea or concept and describe how each of the design's components could be assembled together. Perspective and isometric drawings can also be exploded.

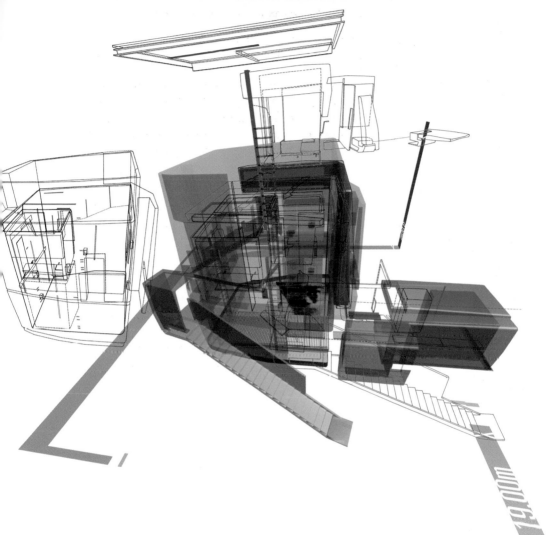

Project: Clone House
Location: Conceptual
Architect: CJ Lim / Studio 8
Date: 1999

The conceptual Clone House
comprises of four identical rooms
and questions the idea of everyday
existence by suggesting a variety
of permutations and configurations.
This exploded perspective drawing
separates aspects of the design
into a series of images identifying
different elements in the structure
such as the roof, walls and
the staircase.

Isometric drawings offer similar three-dimensional views to those of axonometric drawings. However, these drawings attempt to make the very technical representation of an axonometric view slightly more accessible and more of a perspective representation.

Isometric images are useful as they place less emphasis on the vertical aspect of the view. They are also easy to interpret because there is a lower eye level in the views they show, which achieves a more realistic three-dimensional representation.

Producing an isometric drawing

The key difference between axonometric and isometric drawings is that the isometric is created from a plan that is redrawn at a 30-degree distortion (as opposed to the 45-degree tilt of a redrawn axonometric plan). Once the plan is redrawn at this angle, an isometric drawing is produced in exactly the same way as an axonometric one (all lines are projected vertically to produce a three-dimensional rendering of the object).

Isometric drawings are not quick to produce, time needs to be taken to draw the plan at the distorted and tricky angle of 30 degrees before the three-dimensional view can be produced. Certain elements, particularly circular shapes, are very difficult to draw in an isometric form.

Isometric drawings can become cut-away or exploded representations to exaggerate aspects of a concept or idea. Variations in colour, texture and shade can also be used to make the image appear more effective.

The advantage with both isometric and axonometric drawings is that they realistically connect with our natural sense of perception and are more immediate interpretations of a building or space. They can be used equally well to describe concepts, buildings or details, and effectively incorporate aspects of exterior, interior, elevation and form in one representation.

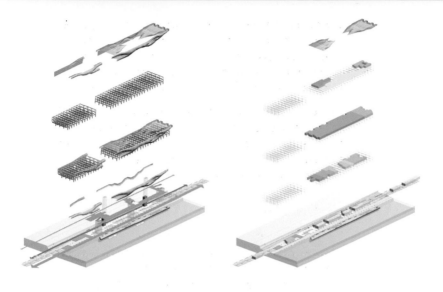

Project: Paris docks
Location: Paris, France
Architects: Jakob + MacFarlane
Date: 2005

This drawing forms part of a series detailing a large redevelopment on the Rive Gauche in Paris. This particular isometric drawing describes the scheme as a riverside journey, overlaid with a series of structures, that are in turn overlaid with a roofscape.

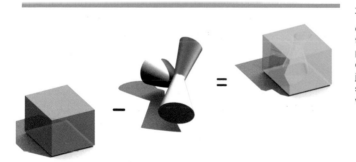

Project: Les Docks, Quai Rimbaud
Location: Lyons, France
Architect: Jakob + MacFarlane
Date: 2005

These CAD models describe the concept of a large exposition building. The building is a solid form that has a shape removed from it leaving a complex void which can be seen and experienced as a space within the building form.

Three-dimensional images can be used both to concentrate the viewer's eye of a particular aspect of a design, or to describe or deconstruct concepts and ideas. There is an essence of both realism and imagined possibilities about these images, and as such they provide an accessible way to better understand a building. In addition to perspective, axonometric and isometric drawings, other forms of three-dimensional representation are also available to the architect.

Fly-through views

Fly-through views are usually produced in a series and are generated from a three-dimensional CAD model. Each image in the series is joined together using editing software to create a film that simulates the viewer 'flying' through the architectural scheme. Fly-through presentations can create an impressive means to view a scheme and understand all its three-dimensional spaces.

Wire-frame models and images

Wire-frame models provide a means to view a building in CAD software. These models only display the outline of the building, but they can still be a useful tool for understanding the building in its early development stages and how it might further develop as a three-dimensional form. A wire-frame image is essentially a transparent image, allowing the viewer to see the building as a three-dimensional outline.

Interior views

Three-dimensional interior views help describe an interior concept or space. These views can be enhanced to show furniture and fitting details, suggest the proposed materials and colour schemes, and incorporate figures to provide a sense of scale. These drawings can also suggest the activities and functions that the design supports.

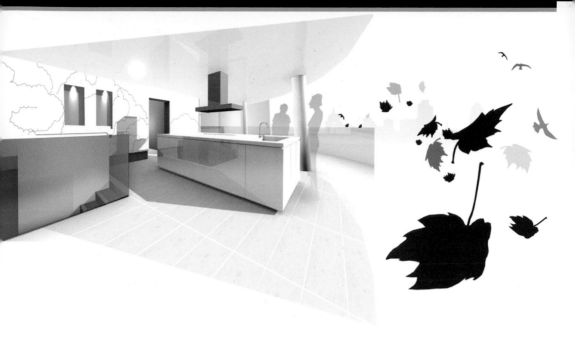

Sectional perspective

Sectional perspectives are a composite representation of section and perspective drawings. They can reveal connections within the design scheme as well as how different areas are intended to work together. In these drawings the descriptions of the suggested activities and view of space in the perspective are extremely important.

Project: 801 Penthouse
Location: London, UK
Architect: Block architecture
Date: 2005

This CAD model was used to create an interior perspective image of a penthouse project in London. The emphasis in the image is placed on the horizontal plane and the objects in the room.

Isometric drawings › **Other applications** › Photomontage and collage

Project: Meridian Delta
Location: London, UK
**Architect: Piercy Conner
Architects**
Date: 2005

This scheme was submitted as
a competition entry for a business
centre and marketing suite in
Greenwich, London in the
shadow of the O2 (previously the
Millennium Dome).

The drawing combines both a
perspective and a section view
through these two spaces, to allow
the viewer to better understand how
the spaces relate to one another and
to their surrounding landscape.
The spaces also contain pictures of
furniture, fittings and people for an
appreciation of scale. These images
were created using MicroStation and
Autodesk 3D Studio Max software.

Cut-away drawings

Cut-away drawings reveal the inside of a building or shape,
which means they can be an effective way to explore the
relationship between the outside and the inside of a building,
or to explain the structure or construction of a building and
how it relates to the original concept or idea. These drawings
are often isometric or axonometric and are presented as a
model with a plane, wall or section removed to give visual
access to the inside of a building or shape.

Three-dimensional images

Project: Sky Blue Aviation
Location: Conceptual
Architects: Matt Swanton /
Format Milton
Date: 2007

Using CAD software this image has been rendered to create a highly-realistic interior view. The reflections, shadows and lighting are impressive and give a sense of depth and greater sense of realism. The furniture also suggests how the space might be used.

Isometric drawings › **Other applications** › Photomontage and collage

Presentation drawings

Presentation drawings can employ the best means of three-dimensional representation to focus on a particular aspect of the architectural idea. Presentation drawings can be produced for a client, the public or for a user group, so they need to communicate the concept with direct relevance to their intended audience and outline the benefits of the architecture for their needs and requirements.

Spatial sequences

A series of three-dimensional drawings can orchestrate a sense of looking around or through an image. Spatial sequences can be used to explain an important aspect of the design concept, such as a route through the building or the means of access and entry to it.

Space and light and order. Those are the things that men need just as much as they need bread or a place to sleep.

Le Corbusier

Project: Clone House
Location: Conceptual
Architects: CJ Lim / Studio 8
Date: 1999

This series of three-dimensional images describe a variety of permutations for CJ Lim's Clone House layout. The layout is a series of four rooms that can be configured in a variety of arrangements. The three-dimensional image, alongside associated plan diagrams, explains these arrangements.

Three-dimensional images

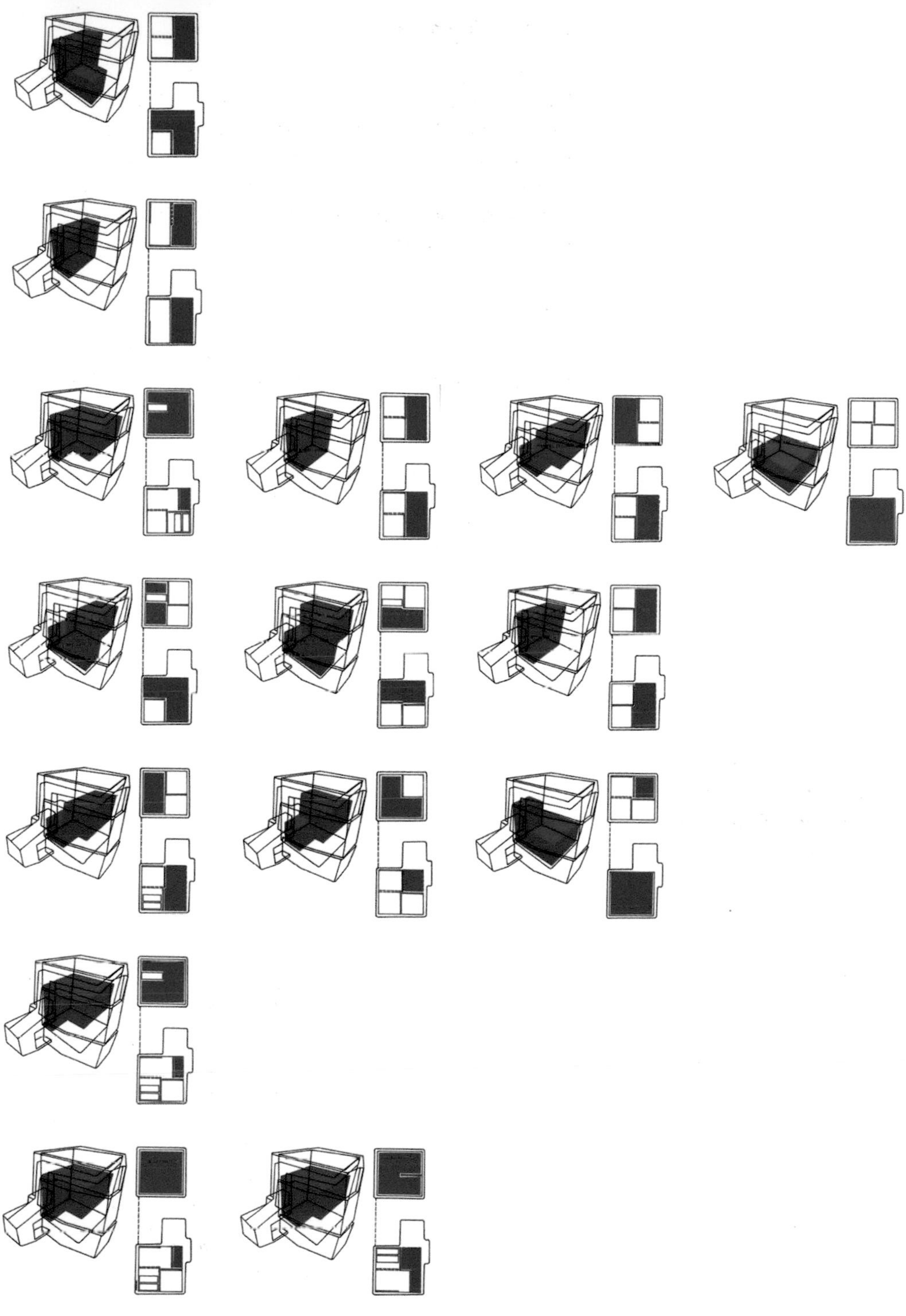

One of the easiest ways to create a sense of reality with an architectural idea is to create photomontage. This technique produces a composite image by cutting, joining and layering a number of other photographs.
In terms of architectural representation, a photomontage image takes an existing view and superimposes onto it a view of a scheme, building or design. A photomontage could be a perspective view or a view of the scheme's plans or elevations.

The photomontage technique can be so seamless that the viewer can 'believe' the proposed idea. The power of photomontage is that it combines actual photographs or impressions of places with imagined ideas of architecture, and the resultant image looks 'real'. Photomontage images are an important means to convince the viewer that the architecture can respond to its site or context effectively.

Traditionally, architectural photomontages were created by photographing a view of a site as well as a physical model of a proposed scheme. These two photographs were then layered on top of one another (the photograph of the model would overlay that of the site), which produced a realistic impression of the scheme. Now, with software programmes such as Photoshop, a digital image of the site can have an image of a CAD model or physical model superimposed on it to create an impression of the final scheme.

If architecture had nothing to do with art, it would be astonishingly easy to build houses, but the architect's task – his most difficult task– is always that of selecting.
Arne Jacobsen

Three-dimensional images

Project: Phare Tower
Location: Paris, France
Architects: Morphosis
Date: 2006

This photomontage image creates
an impressive 'real' view of the
proposed Phare Tower scheme.
It describes the impact the building
will have on its immediate context,
the scale of the new building and
suggests how the form will look
against the skyline.

Collage

Collage derives from the French word 'coller' (to stick).
This is a technique that produces a composite image by the
arranging, layering and sticking of various materials (such as
photographs or fabric swatches) to a backing. Artists such as
George Braque (1882–1963) and Pablo Picasso (1881–1973)
both used collage to juxtapose images and objects in order
to create abstract works of art.

Collaging is used by architects to create a layered image.
These layers may be visual fragments of proposed or
existing sites, buildings or objects, and may include a plan,
perspective and digital images and two- and three-
dimensional drawings in the same composite visual.
Collages offer a much more abstract representation of an
idea than photomontages. A collage is often more suggestive
of a reality; an architect using a collage representation of their
idea does not intend it to be a photorealistic impression.

Sketching in perspective requires an understanding of some basic drawing rules. To sketch well in perspective, it is important to allow time to look at the space you intend to draw and determine its vanishing point(s). A good perspective sketch will be proportionally correct. The ability to convey the relationship of different elements within the image and their relative scale is crucial.

Project: Blackpool people's playground
Location: Blackpool, UK
Architect: dRMM
Date: 2007

These perspective images are used to create a dramatic impression of a building concept by over-emphasising the sense of movement and using exaggerated views.

These early sketches display a series of pavilions for a café/restaurant. The seating areas can move creating many different types of outdoor performance spaces. These perspectives show one such view that the spectator can achieve.

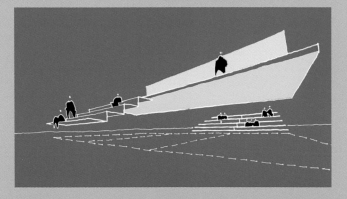

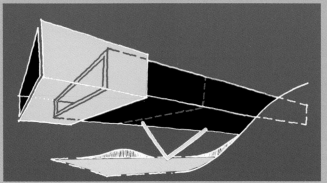

Sketching in perspective

This exercise will explain how to sketch well in perspective. You will need a sketchbook, pencils and pens and you will need to find a place to sketch in single-point perspective. A good option is to find a long view through a room or along a street. Remember, at this stage, it is better to choose a simple space and concentrate on getting the outline correct than to be over-ambitious.

1 Create a grid in your sketchbook that is approximately 10cm squared. This grid will act as a reference plane for you.

2 Use a pencil to draw a vertical line.

3 Draw your view; remember it needs to be proportionally correct so take some time and care. However, remember that this is a sketch so scale is not necessary.

4 Draw a horizontal line to suggest a horizon, ensuring it is at eye level.

5 Draw a vertical line through the centre of the horizontal line. The point at which the two lines intersect is the vanishing point.

6 Now draw (as single lines) all the sight lines that connect back to this point. These lines will define the shape of the space.

7 When you are happy with this outline, sketch in more detail. Don't use rulers and draw lightly in pencil at first, adding more detail with pen later.

Applying a collage technique can further develop the image you have produced. Cutting out pictures of people from some old magazine pages and incorporating them in your sketch can suggest a sense of scale and lend a sense of reality to the image.

Incorporating different material finishes can also add tactile, tonal, or contrasting qualities to the sketch and may even suggest the types of materials that might be used in the final scheme.

Project: Bridge proposal
Location: Hull, UK
Architect: Design Engine
Dates: 2006

This is a competition project for a new bridge in Hull that was designed to open and close in different conditions. This image is generated from a computer-animated model, which demonstrates that the design is intended to open and close. The image was used as part of a film animation demonstrating the movement of the bridge. Computer animation can now present real-time movement as part of a film sequence to provide an incredibly realistic effect.

Modelling allows an architect to explore an idea in a three-dimensional form. Models communicate an architectural idea in an accessible way, immediately showing aspects of scale, form and material. A model can be produced as a full-size prototype of an element (such as a door or window) at the scale of a room, or at the scale of a city (in the form of an urban model). Physical models allow an idea to be explored in greater depth, as certain elements of the scheme or their scale may not be understood until they are seen in the context of a model form.

CAD visualisations offer impressively realistic models that can allow the viewer to choose how they move through a building. CAD models can be used to develop complex forms in the design process, allowing shapes to evolve and explore a range of forms.

Physical models were a popular device in the Renaissance period (during the early fifteenth and early seventeenth centuries in different regions of Europe), and were often relied upon as the sole means of describing an architectural idea. Drawings became the main method for architectural expression during the Beaux-Arts period (during the late nineteenth and early twentieth centuries), but from the mid 1900s, architects once again began to see the benefits of physical models as a means to communicate and shape their ideas. Antonio Gaudí for example, famously used models to help develop the complex structural shapes of Barcelona's La Sagrada Familia cathedral.

Even in today's digital world, with the advances of CAD technologies, the physical model still has an important place. It has a texture and physical presence that can be interrogated and understood. It can be viewed from many directions and suggest materiality and form.

A physical model can be made at any stage of the architectural design process, from initial concept right up to the presentation of the finished scheme. However, different 'types' of physical models tend to be used at different stages of the design process. Whatever the 'type', critical considerations when producing a physical model are scale, materials and the model's relationship to the design concept.

Concept models

A concept model will describe an idea in simple terms in order to clearly communicate the underlying architectural concept. It may be that the choice of material or use of colour is crucial for this type of model in order to isolate and exaggerate the idea and ensure it is clearly and correctly understood. At this stage of the design process massing models, which explore architectural form, are a useful type of concept model as they can be quickly built to scale using materials such as foam, wood or card, and provide an understanding of the relationship between the different site areas.

**Project: Theatrum Gedanense,
Location: Gdansk Poland
Architect: Design Engine
Date: 2005**

The scheme provides a new
interpretation of Gdansk's
Elizabethan theatre by use of new
building technology, environmental
systems and auditoria design.
However, all of these elements are
incorporated to complement the
inherent familiarity and intimacy
of the old scale and proportions.
These concept models demonstrate
the impact the building will have on
the surrounding site.

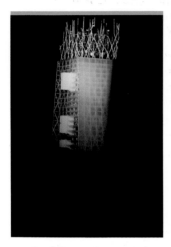

Project: Phare Tower
Location: Paris, France
Architects: Morphosis
Date: 2006

The Phare Tower (or Tour Phare in French) is a planned 300-meter-tall skyscraper designed as a green building to be built in the Parisian district of La Défense. The building was designed by architect Thom Mayne, and is scheduled to be completed in 2012.

The French word 'phare' means lighthouse and the building has been designed to act as a beacon on the Parisian skyline. This model for the scheme has been made to describe the translucent nature of the cladding or skin of the building. It reveals in places the skeletal structure of the building and appears almost organic in form.

Development models

Development models are produced at various stages of the design process and are intended to align the scheme's concept with the brief's specifications. These models can inform stages of the design process and may change radically as the scheme progresses. They offer the quickest means for solving and exploring three-dimensional problems and exploiting the potential for design development (as the viewer can look over, through, inside and outside a development model). A development model can be used equally well as a basis for discussion between the client and the design team or as a means for testing a particular aspect of the scheme.

Illuminated models

Illuminated models can create an impressive effect by incorporating miniature bulbs, fibre optics, transparent or semi-opaque materials. These models are often used to highlight particular aspects of a scheme or design.

As well as creating an impressive aesthetic, illuminated models can lend themselves well to representing certain projects. For example, buildings that are intended to be used heavily in the evening (such as theatres, restaurants or bars) will have a different physical presence at night than they do in the day, and an illuminated model can suggest the impact that the lit building will have on its immediate environment.

Presentation models

These are models of the final scheme. They may be used for the purposes of public consultation before a scheme starts or they may provide an overview of the finished building for a client.

The scale of the presentation model and the volume of surrounding architecture or landscape that it displays needs to be carefully considered. If, for example, a project relates to particular reference points in the surrounding area, such as an important building, road or route, then these should be included in the model as they will affect the development of the design.

The materials used to construct the model, and information about how these relate to the finished scheme, will provide a greater sense of realism to a presentation model.

Contrary to what you may think, you don't require complicated specialist tools or materials to make physical models. Professional model makers may use sophisticated machinery to obtain impressive and highly accurate finished models, but most architects use slightly more rudimentary tools to construct their own models.

Tools

To make models, the basic tools required are a cutting mat, a metal ruler, scissors, knives and hot-wire cutters.

A cutting mat provides a base on which to cut materials. This is normally made of rubber, but a piece of hardboard or other tough surface can also be used. Rubber cutting mats have a grid printed onto them to allow straight lines to be cut quickly and easily.

Metal rules provide a clear edge to cut against and will prevent the knife from slicing into the rule when in use (an advantage that a plastic rule won't have). Never use a scale rule to cut against because the knife will score its edge.

Sharp knives are important for cutting materials cleanly and precisely. The cut of the material is important, so take time and make your incisions carefully. If a material is cut at an angle it won't look like a clean edge when it is joined with another piece.

A scalpel blade is the most useful knife as it will be extremely sharp. It needs to be used with extreme care, as too much pressure will cause the blade to snap. Any knife work needs to be done in good light, cutting slowly and carefully.

Scissors can only be used for cutting paper and very thin card. If using wood as a modelling material, then tools such as a bench saw, table saw or jigsaw are necessary for accurate cutting.

Hot-wire cutters slice through foam accurately and leave a clean edge. Their fine wire is heated electrically, and the wire's malleable quality allows shapes drawn onto the foam to be cut quickly by pushing the material against the wire. This is a fast way to make a model of a city; a map of the area can be drawn onto the foam, which is then cut to produce block shapes.

Modelling

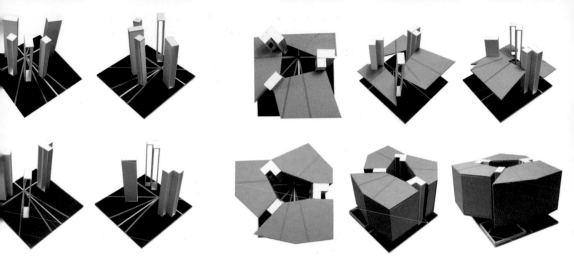

Materials

The choice of material used to construct any model will relate to the speed with which the model needs to be made, the stage of the design idea and what the model is aiming to explore or explain. To decide which materials to incorporate in your model it is necessary to consider whether it needs to be representative of the 'real' materials that are to be used in the design scheme, or whether you want to produce a 'neutral' model, which concentrates on the building form and mass.

'Real' models can represent a material quality of the architectural idea. In some cases the model could be made of a similar material to that intended for the finished building, however this is not always appropriate or practical.

Sometimes it may only be necessary to demonstrate a particular characteristic of the building's material in the model form. For example, if an architectural design incorporates a metal roof that is intended to be highly reflective, this could be emphasised by using metal, whilst other materials may be representative of the building's form.

Project: Chichester Museum
Location: Chichester, UK
Designer: Paul Craven Bartle
Date: 2007

The design for this project began as a series of sculptural towers, which served as access to the museum and housed stairs and lifts. The building form then developed around these elements as a series of platforms or levels. The models were photographed at various stages of the development of the scheme to explain how the design progressed.

Physical models › **Physical modelling equipment** › Model scales

Models that are made of materials such as card or wood can be described as neutral. The final scheme will almost always be made of other materials, but neutral materials will sufficiently represent the mass and form of the scheme on its site.

When choosing the material for your model, it can be a good idea to consider any surrounding buildings on the site. Proposed and existing scheme models will read more clearly if each is differentiated by material type or colour. Also, the scale of the model will have an impact on the materials it is to be built from. A model showing a city will have less detail than one showing an interior, and more detailed models may have layers of material applied to them to create interest or a sense of realism.

Card

Card is available in many weights and colours and can be cut accurately with a knife to achieve a straight edge. These properties make it a versatile material for model making. Corrugated card can be self-supporting, which makes it a good material for a model's walls or roof. Also, the corrugated edge can be used to suggest particular finishes on the building.

Foam board

Foam board describes a piece of foam that is sandwiched between two thin pieces of card. It is available in a variety of weights, which means that it is a useful material for representing different wall widths. It is also a fairly sturdy material, so on smaller models is self-supporting. Coloured foam board can be used to suggest different material finishes.

Polystyrene and styrofoam

Polystyrene is very flexible and can be cut and shaped easily to create organic forms. Styrofoam is a board material that can be easily cut, shaped, glued and painted. It has a finely textured surface that provides a smooth finish for model making. It is also lightweight, easy to handle and reusable.

Project: John Roan School
Location: London, UK
Architect: Architecture Plb
(model by David Grandorge)
Date: 2007

Models made from wood can be easily adapted and developed. This model shows part of a scheme proposal for a school relocation in London. The wood adds a variety of colours and textures to the mode.

Wood

Models made from wood can be easily adapted and developed. Most commonly used for model making, balsa wood comes from a tropical tree source and is very light (it has a density that is a third of other hardwoods), so it is easy to cut, which is good for creating accurate models.

Other woods can be used to provide particular finishes. Cork, for example, can be used to give a carpet-like effect to a surface, which is useful for city-scale models.

Wood can be finely sanded and varnished to achieve a range of finishes, and using different woods in varying grains or colours will affect the appearance of your model.

Project: Queen Mary University
Location: London, UK
Architect: Alsop Architects
Date: 2005

Alsop Architects' designs for this
Queen Mary University proposal
contrast strong three-dimensional
forms in a structural framework.
This model is made from perspex;
as it is a transparent material it allows
the structural shapes to be read
through the building frame.

Metal

In model making, metal can be used in sheet form to suggest various building finishes, wall cladding or roofing. The sheets can be made from aluminium, copper, brass or steel, and can be perforated or corrugated and in mesh or flat-sheet form.

Transparent materials

These can lend interesting qualities to a physical model. Perspex and acrylic can be completely transparent or have a semi-opaque finish, and coloured acrylics can be used to good effect in model making. Using lights to illuminate transparent material will exaggerate the effect of the design's features.

Scale and finishes

Introducing objects for which we understand the scale will make a model appear more realistic and help the viewer to understand the proportions of the architecture. These objects might be model figures, cars or trees – any elements that are immediately accessible to the viewer.

The finish should be an important consideration at all stages of the model's construction. Time needs to be taken when cutting materials to ensure that they are cut accurately, and care taken when assembling the pieces. This care will ensure that the model is considered as an important part of the whole design presentation.

Notes on adhesives

Different materials will require different adhesives to allow them to fix properly. Always ensure that the appropriate glues are used, if not the model will not stick together or the glue may mark or even dissolve the material of the model.

- Some adhesives will dry to a transparent finish, which may be important.

- Adhesive spray allows pieces to be stuck together and then repositioned. This is useful for fixing paper and thin card.

- PVA (polyvinyl acetate) glue is general-purpose glue that is good for porous materials such as wood.

- Glue dots can be placed on pieces of material that are then pushed together producing a clean finish.

- Contact adhesives, as the name suggests, affix materials on contact.

- Specialist glues are needed for certain materials. Balsa cement, for example, is good for balsa and other lightweight woods.

- Tape is a useful tool for holding glued pieces together while they fix. Masking tape won't leave marks on the modelling materials and double-sided tape allows two materials to fix together quickly.

- Glue guns give a quick, fast-drying effect.

Although some physical models take an abstract form and so are not to scale (similarly initial architectural models, such as concept models, explore ideas of material and form and these models may not use scale), the use of scale can offer an advantage in model making as it allows an appreciation of the real or perceived size of a proposed building or space.

As an architectural idea develops the scale at which it is investigated changes:

- An urban model showing the masterplan of a city will be produced at 1:2500 or 1:1250 scale. This is roughly the same scale as a map and allows aspects of the city to be read in connection with one another.

- A model of a large building will relate to its site at 1:500 scale and as the idea develops the scale of investigation changes until it becomes a model at 1:50 or 1:20 scale, which is approximately the size of a standard room.

- Models produced at 1:10, 1:5 or 1:2 scale are normally used to describe the material details of a building or space or how its component parts will join and fit together.

- Some physical models are made at actual or real size. If a building component, for example a window, frame or roof, has to be specially tested then it may be manufactured and reproduced as a full-size prototype. Real-size models allow close examination of the proposed building component in its 'true' form.

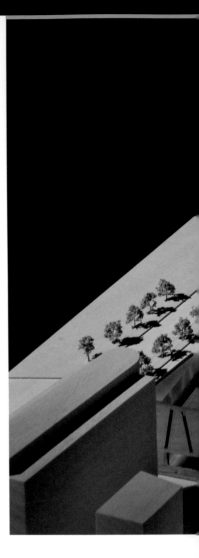

Project: John Roan School
Location: London, UK
Architect: Architecture Plb
(model by David Grandorge)
Date: 2007

This model outlines a proposal for a
school project in London. The school
will form the focus of an urban
masterplan combining community,
residential and commercial
developments.

The model uses different types of
timber to differentiate between the
existing and the proposed buildings.

The various types of wood also
identify with the proposed
construction materials for the
elevation cladding and the roof.

Physical modelling equipment › **Model scales**

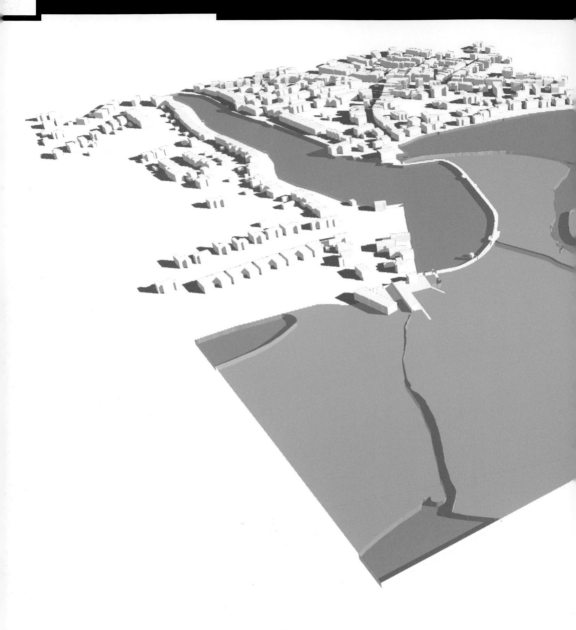

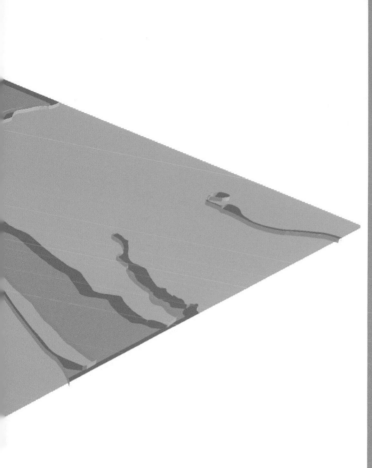

Photographing models

Although a model may well be intended to be viewed and investigated in three-dimensional form, if it is photographed then it can also be included in a portfolio of work, or in the creation of CAD images or photomontage and collage images. Important considerations when photographing models are:

• Stage the views and use a neutral background such as a white or black sheet that will contrast with the model.

• If possible, try and photograph your model outdoors using the sky as a backdrop. This can add to the overall realism of the piece.

• Consider light and shadow falling on the model. Orientate it as it should be in reality and this will make the model a truer representation of the scheme.

• Ensure that there aren't any objects or elements in the frame of the photograph that will affect the scale illusion of the model.

• Photograph the model from all angles, as overview images and then zoom in to capture details. This will provide a range of views of the model for use in other presentations.

• In some cases it can be useful to photograph the different stages of the model's construction as this will show the stages of development of the idea.

Project: Emsworth Activity Centre
Location: Emsworth, UK
Designer: Khalid Saleh
Date 2007

The site for this activity centre is on the water's edge and is adjacent to a relatively dense residential area. This CAD site model offers an important description of the site and explains its critical location. The model also describes the surrounding landscape and the variable water depth, which is an important factor for this design.

Physical modelling equipment › **Model scales** › CAD models

CAD models

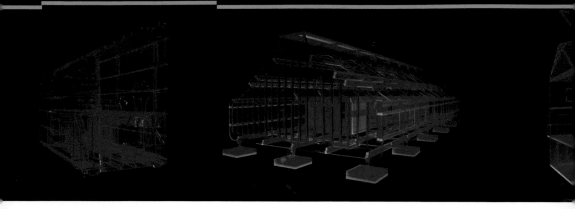

Project: Wire frame models
Architects: Piercy Connor
Architects
Date: 2006

These images represent architectural
ideas in the form of wire frame
models. The buildings appear as a
series of transparent frames, without
any surrounding cladding or material.
A wire frame model is a useful device
when developing a design idea, and
can also create an impressive
presentation image.

**Computer aided design (CAD) assists the generation
of two-dimensional plan, section and elevation drawings
as well as the creation of three-dimensional interactive
models.**

Originally developed in the 1960s for commercial application
in the aerospace and electronic industries, CAD was further
developed for desktop computer use during the 1980s.
Autodesk and AutoCAD were the first CAD software
programmes developed for PCs (in 1981). Macintosh-based
systems were developed and made available later in the
decade. Today most CAD software programmes work across
both platforms

Generally CAD schemes are 'drawn' on screen using a
mouse, but some systems use a pen and graphics tablet.
In such systems the CAD software renders lines and points
made by the stylus onto the computer screen.

Creating CAD models offers the architect the possibility to
show the scheme at any stage during its development, to
quickly adapt a design and respond to changes in the project
brief, and to show impressive graphics and a range of interior
and exterior views of a building or space.

Modelling

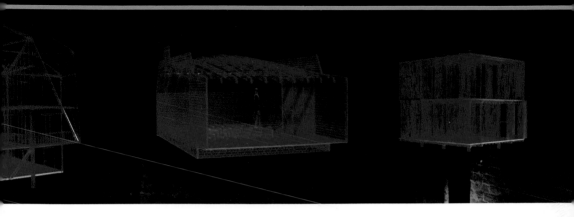

Rapid prototyping

Rapid prototyping refers to a modelling process that can fabricate a physical scale model using three-dimensional CAD data. What is commonly considered to be the first rapid prototyping technique, stereolithography, was developed in 1986 by 3D Systems (based in Valencia, CA, USA).

Rapid prototyping is also referred to as solid free-form manufacturing, computer automated manufacturing and layered manufacturing. All four labels essentially refer to the same workflow; a computer is connected to machinery that interprets the data and creates the three-dimensional model. The model is then produced by the machine using layers of paper, plastic or other materials. Rapid prototyping means that the exact same model exists in both virtual (CAD) and physical form.

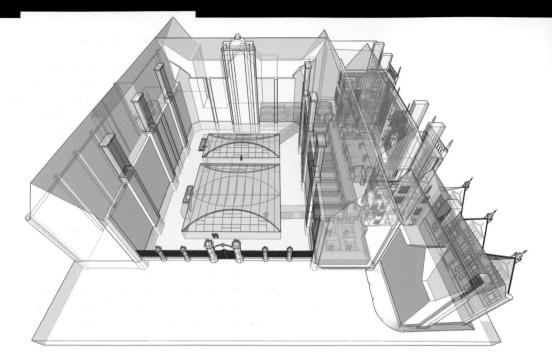

To make a CAD model effectively, it is useful to have access to a range of different pieces of software. CAD software can be broadly categorised as programs that offer the functionality to create two-dimensional drawings, three-dimensional models and hybrids that produce both.

When using CAD software it is important to experiment with different applications as each will have varying advantages, from sophisticated film and editing possibilities to rendering packages that produce realistic impressions of any building material. Most drawing packages are constantly updated and reissued as new versions of the programme, offering improved tools and associated facilities. Over the last few years advances in CAD software functionality has created the possibility for impressively realistic models.

CAD at different stages of the design process

The production of CAD drawings and models should not be considered as a replacement for the creation of physical models, freehand drawings or sketches. Instead CAD software can facilitate the development of shapes and forms that could not be created via plan, section and elevation drawings. As such it is a tool to be used at critical points during the design process.

The first of these points is at the initial massing stage of a project. CAD models can be used here to create an overall impression of the scale of a proposed building, and suggest its outline form as well as its likely impact on the surrounding context.

A second key advantage is that interior CAD models can show a 'fly through' series of images (see pages 140–141), moving the viewer through a 'film' of the proposed scheme. Many CAD software programmes offer the functionality to both direct and edit a fly through sequence of views from a model.

Finally, using CAD rendering packages means that material finishes can be scanned and applied (just like wallpaper) onto the models. These packages can also offer lighting options, projecting shadow inside and around a building, which can create an even greater sense of realism.

Project: Oxford University examination hall
(facing page and right)
Location: Oxford, UK
Architect: Design Engine
Date: 2006

Models can be used to describe concepts in a variety of ways. Here, Design Engine architects use a wire frame model to create a transparent frame from which to generate views of the space of the examination hall in Oxford University.

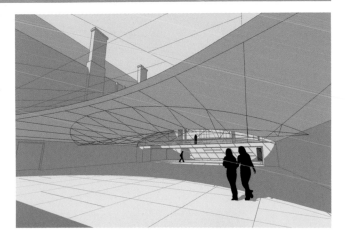

Greater possibilities

As well as allowing impressive visuals, CAD software has afforded a new type of architecture. Complex forms, which were not previously possible, can now be modelled in CAD programmes and their form, structure and materials tested. CAD technology is critical for these sort of architectural forms; quite simply, physical models cannot fully explore such ideas sufficiently enough to convince the client and engineers of the possibility of the design.

Specific CAD applications are used for modelling these new architectural forms. VectorWorks is a drawing package that is very useful for creating two-dimensional plan, section and elevation drawings. It also offers a three-dimensional modelling package.

ArchiCAD originated as a three-dimensional modelling package, but now has the functionality to produce two-dimensional drawings as well. It can be used with additional software to create realistic material finishes and fly through views of the scheme.

AutoCAD is universally available and is used by many architects and engineers as their standard drawing software.

Google SketchUp can be used to build and modify three-dimensional models quickly and easily. If used in conjunction with Google Earth, SketchUp allows you to place your models on site using actual coordinates and share them via Google 3D Warehouse.

Rendering packages, such as artlantis or Autodesk 3D Studio Max, work with other drawing programmes to create impressive material and colour finishes to models.

Project: The Visitor Centre, Hardwick Park
Location: Durham, UK
Architect: Design Engine
Date: 2006

These CAD images form part of a proposal for a new visitor interpretation centre. The centre's form is designed using bridge-building technology; each skeletal sector is clad in corten steel for a naturally protected 'rust' finish.

The concept of the visitor centre is connected to the natural form of a conker; in this way the pavilion sits as a 'found' object in a wooded site, imitating natural and organic forms.

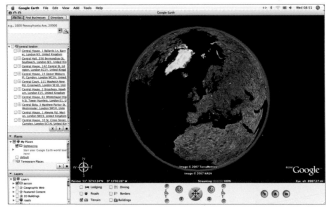

Google SketchUp and Google Earth

Google SketchUp is available to download from www.sketchup.com. It is an easy to use and intuitive piece of software that allows three-dimensional shapes to be formed quickly. Once the form has been created, SketchUp has the functionality to allow apertures to be created in the shape to suggest doors and windows.

Google Earth software allows any location in the world to be viewed as an aerial photograph, though some areas display more detail than others. Google Earth can be used in conjunction with SketchUp, which means that you can draw a form in SketchUp and place that form on a location image generated in Google Earth. This allows you to create images that not only show a structural concept, but also allow it to be viewed in a realistic context.

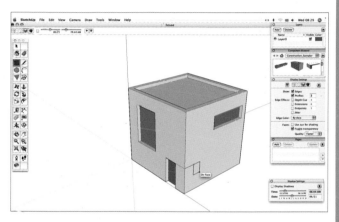

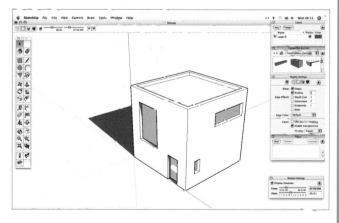

Drawing file formats

Many software programmes support the transfer of data and drawings between one platform and another. If the drawings are saved as neutral file types then they can be accessed across programmes.

- DWG files originated in the AutoCAD software package, but have since become the standard file type to exchange drawing files. The DXF file format is a variant. Most CAD programmes (such as AutoCAD, Autodesk, MicroStation, VectorWorks and ArchiCAD) use the DWG format.

- Drawings can also be saved as JPEG files and transferred from one piece of software to another. JPEG stands for Joint Photographic Experts Group, which is the name of the committee that created the standard.

- STL is a file format native to stereolithography CAD software.

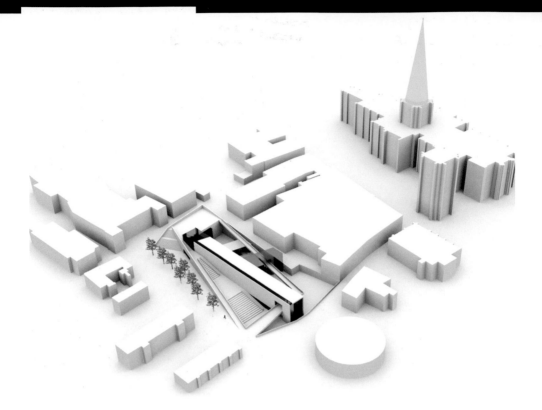

Whether a CAD or physical model is generated to represent, explain and explore an architectural scheme, the advantage it has (over any drawn form) is that it allows many views of a building to be considered.

Many CAD software packages offer the facility to explore a three-dimensional model using 'fly through' techniques. This technique describes the capturing of individual views from within the model and editing them to form a series of connected images that render as if one is 'flying through' the building or space.

The fly through technique can also be applied to a physical model by photographing it from a variety of angles and then assembling the images to suggest a journey through the proposed scheme that best describes the architectural concept.

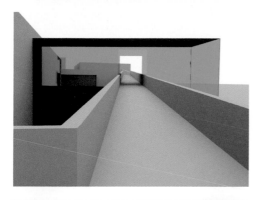

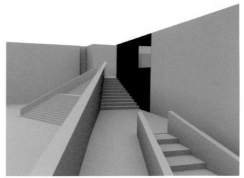

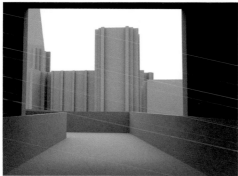

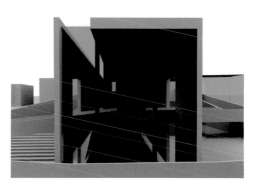

Project: Chichester Museum
Location Chichester, UK
Designer: Khalid Saleh
Date: 2007

These images show a sequential
series of CAD models for a museum
design. The museum's site is
adjacent to an important cathedral
precinct and this location informed
the concept for the proposal. The
spire of the cathedral, for example,
was to be visible at various points
in the scheme.

The 'fly through' CAD images allow
the journey through the scheme
and the associated views to be
understood. The images were
created using a range of software.
Initially the scheme was drawn in
VectorWorks software; it was then
imported into SketchUp to create
three-dimensional models, and was
finally rendered in 3ds Max. The
perspective images were edited in
Photoshop software.

Project: Concept model
Architect: Alsop Architects
Date: 2006

This is an abstract physical model, it is not to scale but concentrates on relative form and use of materials to describe the idea.

One of the important aspects of architectural design is the idea that form and shape can be influenced by many different things. Painting, and abstract painting in particular, has the potential to be understood as a three-dimensional form and has been a source of inspiration for many architectural ideas and concepts.

Gerrit Rietveld, for example, created architecture that was connected to the work of artists such as Piet Mondrian, who used colour to suggest form in his paintings.

Transforming two dimensions into three

This exercise will look at a two-dimensional image and, through a series stages, will interpret it as a three-dimensional model. This process is representative of the design thinking involved when creating architecture.

1   Start by looking at an abstract painting. Take time to observe and understand it.

2   Now sketch any images or shapes that you can see within it. Quickly draw a range of sketches that represent your different interpretations of the painting.

3   When the sketches are complete, look at them and determine the different shapes or forms within each one.

4   Now make these forms quickly using card or paper and fixing them with tape. Doing so should generate a series of models that connect with your sketches.

5   Select the initial sketch model that holds the most interest. Think about its shape and begin to develop it further, perhaps by using more or different materials, or by altering its size orientation.

6   Create a final piece that responds to your investigations of scale, materials and form.

7   Finally, assemble the initial painting, with your sketches, sketch models and your final piece. Collectively these will represent your personal design process in transforming a two-dimensional image into a three-dimensional form.

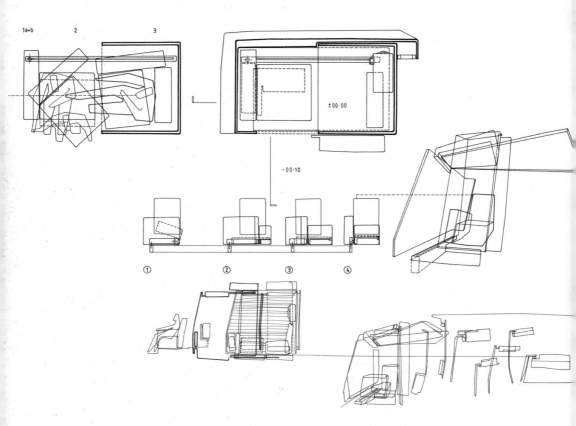

1a+b   2   3

±00·00

- 00·10

① ② ③ ④

In architectural design, layout and presentation form a critical part of the design process because the architect relies heavily on the successful representation of their ideas to convince the viewer of the feasibility of their scheme. The architect needs to create graphically seductive images that are both interesting and engaging, and describe the proposed scheme so well that the viewers can envisage themselves in this future space.

Appropriateness of the presentation type to the design concept needs to be carefully considered and balanced. Drawings such as plans, sections and elevations explain a building in a measured and defined form. Other drawings can be more emotive and suggest an environment for, or an experience of, the architecture. Minimal, modern building proposals are often described by minimal drawings that use simple lines and plain backgrounds, and classically embellished building proposals will be described by crafted, decorated drawings. Appropriateness of presentation is determined by the drawing's relationship to the architectural style.

Layout is also part of the design process. Arranging or organising drawings so that they tell the story of the architecture in a considered and coherent way is vital if the architect is to successfully communicate their design proposal. A 'set' of architectural drawings (here this term is used to imply the connection between individual drawings to describe the architecture as coherently as possible) must place the building in its physical and design context.

Project: Glass Booth
Location: Conceptual
Architect: CJ Lim / Studio 8
Date: 2006

A series of associated plans, elevations and perspective images describe this scheme. The black and red lines help distinguish the architectural form from the figure. The combination of different forms of representation provide a coherent description of the architectural idea.

ISO paper sizes
(plus rounded inch values)

Format A series

Size	mm x mm	in x in
A0	841 x 1189	33.1 x 46.8
A1	594 x 841	23.4 x 33.1
A2	420 x 594	16.5 x 23.4
A3	297 x 420	11.7 x 16.5
A4	210 x 297	8.3 x 11.7
A5	148 x 210	5.8 x 8.3
A6	105 x 148	4.1 x 5.8

Format B series

Size	mm x mm	in x in
A0	1000 x 1414	39.4 x 55.7
A1	707 x 1000	27.8 x 39.
A2	500 x 707	19.7 x 27.8
A3	353 x 500	13.9 x 19.7
A4	250 x 353	9.8 x 13.9
A5	176 x 250	6.9 x 9.8
A6	125 x 176	4.9 x 6.9

Format C series

Size	mm x mm	in x in
A0	917 x 1297	36.1 x 51.1
A1	648 x 917	25.5 x 36.1
A2	58 x 648	18.0 x 25.5
A3	324 x 458	12.8 x 18.0
A4	229 x 324	9.0 x 12.8
A5	162 x 229	6.4 x 9.0
A6	114 x 162	4.5 x 6.4

The layout of architectural images will affect the viewer's interpretation of a design concept. A set of plan, elevation and section drawings can be arranged to create a three-dimensional form of a building proposal, and the way in which these drawings are organised is important; arranged correctly they tell the 'right' story.

The plans serve as maps, explaining the relationships between rooms, spaces and routes. The sections, when read in conjunction with the plans, explain the height of and vertical relationships between the building's spaces. The elevations explain the relationships between the doors and openings described in the plans. To tell the story of the architecture correctly these drawings should be carefully presented so that their inter-relationships are clearly evident.

Paper size

Many architectural drawings are created in CAD software programmes that can produce images at any format and size. The decision of what size to render these images at will be determined to their printed format, which is in turn governed by where and how the work will be presented.

Larger formats (such as A0, A1 and A2 sheets) are useful for presentation drawings for an exhibition or public examination. The smaller A3 and A4 formats are quicker and cheaper to produce, but they are limited in the amount of information that they can communicate; there is only so much content that can be contained on these sheet sizes.

Portrait or landscape?

Once the paper size has been determined, the orientation of the sheets needs to be decided upon.

Landscape format describes a horizontal orientation, portrait format describes a vertical one. This terminology finds its origins in the fine arts; landscape paintings (as the name suggests) often depicted landscape scenes and the horizon, whereas the tradition of portrait painting was characterised by depicting a human figure or a face within a vertical frame.

The choice of 'frame' for architectural drawings will be influenced by similar factors. A building situated within the landscape, for example, will better relate to a horizontal frame, whereas plans for a skyscraper will sit better in a vertical frame.

Traditionally, all architectural drawings were displayed in landscape orientation. Drawings were produced on landscape boards and elevations were produced as horizontal strips that were linked to the building's plans, allowing a clear connection between the drawings on the sheet.

Nowadays, architectural drawings need to project a 'possible reality'; real spaces that have possible functions, lifestyles or experiences attached to them. In a sense, architectural drawings can be used as a form of advertising, projecting the architectural scheme as a lifestyle choice to the viewer. Very often these presentation drawings need to incorporate both the practical, measured architectural elements as well as exciting inspirational visuals.

ANSI paper sizes

In 1995, the American National Standards Institute (ANSI) adopted ANSI/ASME Y14.1, which defined a regular series of paper sizes. This series is somewhat similar to the ISO paper size standard in that cutting a sheet in half would produce two sheets of the next smaller size.

Name	in x in	mm x mm	Similar ISO size
ANSI A	8 x 11	279 x 216	A4
ANSI B	11 x 17	432 x 279	A3
ANSI C	17 x 22	539 x 432	A2
ANSI D	22 x 34	864 x 539	A1
ANSI E	34 x 44	1118 x 864	A0

In addition to the ANSI system, there is a corresponding series of paper sizes used for architectural purposes. This series also shares the property that bisecting each size produces two of the size below.

Name	in x in	mm x mm
Arch A	12 x 9	305 x 229
Arch B	18 x 12	457 x 305
Arch C	24 x 18	610 x 457
Arch D	36 x 24	914 x 610
Arch E	48 x 36	1219 x 914
Arch E1	42 x 30	1067 x 762

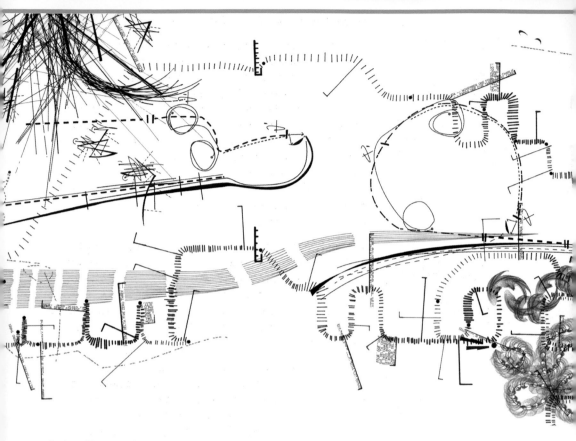

Project: Chambers Street
Architect: David Mathias
Date: 2004

This map is part of a 'choreography of a street' project and it relates to both a specific place and a particular journey. The map brings together abstract drawings and lines to form a complete composition. The drawings use lines in different ways, sometimes they are solid and continuous and at other times they are broken. We can interpret this image as a formalised drawing or as an abstract image.

Layout and presentation

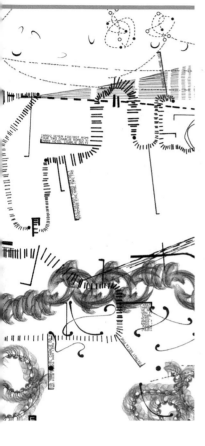

Organising sets of drawings

The organisation of measured drawings requires careful editing to ensure the clarity of their presentation. It is possible to have a set of drawings that incorporates several different scales; however, unless they are all absolutely necessary it is usually better to limit the number of differently scaled images. For example, a location plan may be produced at 1:1250 in order to locate the position of the project in the context of its surrounding environment. This introduces one level of scale so it may then be simpler to ensure that the rest of the drawings are produced at a building scale of 1:200 or 1:100 so the viewer only has to read two or three levels across the whole presentation.

When assembling a range of drawings it can be useful to sketch out the layout of each as a thumbnail image (a small, not-to-scale sketch) to highlight the relationships between each of the drawings and the information they contain. This can help plan the organisation and ensure that the scheme is communicated correctly and that the drawings complement one another.

Collectively, the drawings need to tell the story of the scheme. As such, concept images should be seen first to explain the origins of the architect's ideas. The location plan also needs to appear at an early age as it describes where the building sits on a site. The site and ground plans should be read next, followed by any other building plans. The plans need to be adjacent to one another so that they can be read together, providing an explanation of the relationships between elements that work vertically within the building and across the scheme's floor plans. All plan drawings should be presented in the same orientation.

Architecture is the learned game, correct and magnificent, of forms assembled in the light.
Le Corbusier

Layout › Graphic presentations

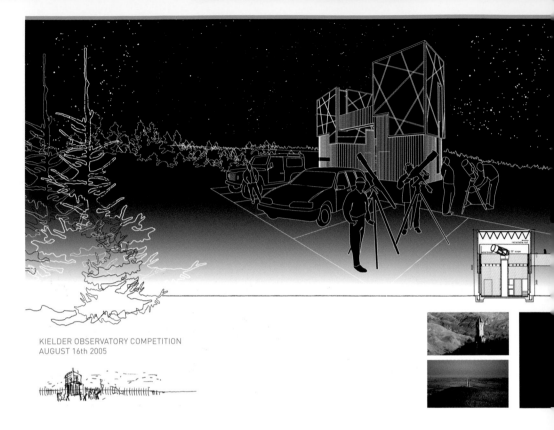

KIELDER OBSERVATORY COMPETITION
AUGUST 16th 2005

Project: Kielder Observatory
Location: Kielder, Scotland
Architect: Block architecture
Date: 2005

This is a layout presentation for a proposed observatory in Kielder, Scotland. The organisation of the layout drawing is thorough, and includes a written synopsis of the scheme, plan, section and elevation drawings, perspective views and photographs of a model.

This provides a range of different ways to understand the scheme. The layout's backdrop image is the night sky, which complements the idea of the observatory, and the images read effectively as white drawings against the black background.

Elevation drawings need to refer back to the plan drawings. Positioning the elevation drawings directly beneath their associated plan is helpful because it allows the viewer to read the connections between, say, the door and window openings on both drawings. Elevation drawing titles should reference their orientation (such as the south- or north-facing elevation), so one can immediately understand which part of the building receives most sunlight.

Any section drawing should clearly correspond to the position on the plan where its 'cut' is taken. This should be indicated on the plan with the title of the section drawing (such as section AA or section BB).

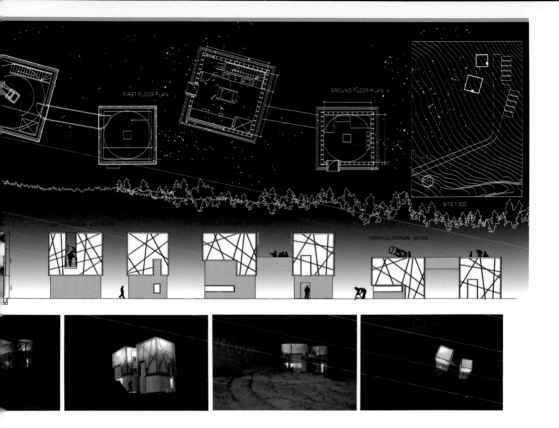

A good visual presentation should not be cluttered, it needs to have sufficient space to allow the information to be easily read and absorbed. The information may be rendered in varying sizes or using different graphic styles and techniques. The drawings must align purposefully as this will help the viewer read the drawings as a collective set.

Project: Queen Mary University
(above and facing page)
Location: London, UK
Architect: Alsop Architects
Date: 2005

This is a heavily annotated freehand drawing of a university building. The drawing explores the relationship of sculptural forms in a structural frame and the visual notes alongside the drawing describe the ideas and possible directions for development of the project. The use of colour on the drawing accents the important elements within the building.

Layout and presentation

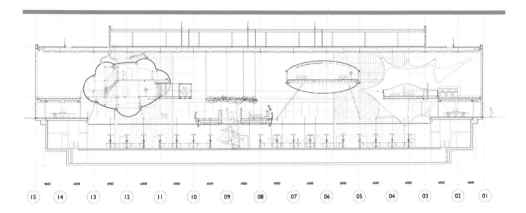

4400	6000	6000	6000	6000	6000	6000	6000	6000	6000	6000	6000	6000	4400	
15	14	13	12	11	10	09	08	07	06	05	04	03	02	01

Project: Queen Mary University
Location: London, UK
Architects: Alsop Architects
Date: 2005

In this section drawing there is
a sense of an internal landscape
within the building as a series of
pods appearing to float in an open
atrium space. The contrast between
the formalised frame of the building
and the sculptural shape of the
pods makes the internal space
a distinctive experience.

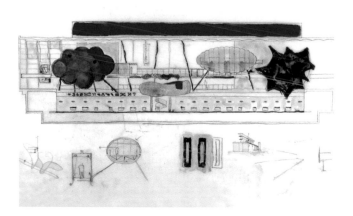

Project: Blackfriars Bridge
Location: London, UK
Architects: CJ Lim / Studio 8
Date: 2007

This collage mixes real images of Blackfriars Bridge with seaside-themed visuals, such as ice cream vans, beach huts and beach balls, combining an understood reality with an imagined fantasy.

The resulting imagined-reality image is powerful and provocative, suggesting a reinvention of the bridge.

The graphic presentation of architectural drawings should complement the design idea. There are many occasions where the presentation of a proposal relies solely on the graphic presentation (such as in examinations or for competition entries). As such the presentation must clearly communicate the architect's idea, concept and intention. To do so requires a balance between the information contained within the drawings and any supplementary text or visuals supporting them. Achieving this balance ensures that the layout of the building design and architectural features can be read easily and accurately.

The style of a graphic presentation can vary by the use of different colours, drawing techniques, sizes or types of imagery and font sizes and styles. Some of these choices can be cleverly made so that the style of the graphic presentation echoes the style of the proposed architecture.

Measured drawings have a scale associated with them, so they need to be reproduced accurately. It should be remembered when composing an architectural presentation that as well as producing seductive graphics, the scheme has to be shown to work practically and functionally.

Layout and presentation

'Imagined-reality' visuals

Imagined-reality visuals are intended to excite and invigorate the viewer. They are impressions of a place or space created by the architect, and as such the use of colour and the creation of a certain sense of drama are important considerations. The layout of a visual element must connect strongly to the content of the image, for example, there may be pictures of activities associated with the proposed architecture that can be included to unite the presentation and the underlying concept. These visuals may form the centrepiece to a series of measured drawings or create a theme for the presentation across a range of laid-out pages.

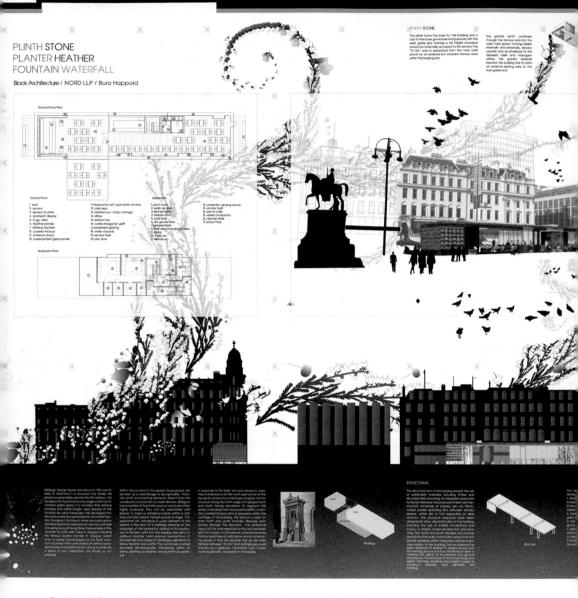

PLINTH STONE
PLANTER HEATHER
FOUNTAIN WATERFALL

Block Architecture / NORD LLP / Buro Happold

Layout and presentation

Project: St George's Square
Location: Glasgow, Scotland
Architect: Block architecture
Date: 2006

This comprehensive presentation explains an idea for an urban square in Glasgow. The bottom half of the drawing is a representation of the street façade, which provides an explanation of the site context and serves as a base for other elements of the drawing.

The concept is further explained with some explanatory text and diagrams, which are presented as a narrative along the base of the drawing.

The perspective drawings convey a three-dimensional impression of the scheme and computer generated images of the site provide a sense of realism.

FOUNTAIN WATERWALL

The glazed skin wraps around the exterior of the café and gives an overall unity to the proposed building, whilst maintaining visual permeability across the square. The glass skin provides an opportunity to introduce "waterwalls" along all 3 external surfaces creating a tranquil café space buffered from the hustle and bustle of the square. The waterwalls suggest the idea that the building envelope becomes a fountain intermittently covered with cascading water.

The reflection and sound of the water will also help change the mood of the building and physicality of the square encouraging people to stop and pause from their day to day activities. The water also acts as a shading device cooling the building in the summer and as a low maintenance, self cleaning façade.

Glass and Water

PLANTER HEATHER

We have drawn from the swelling language of planted stands within the square by proposing a green roof. The roof would be planted different types of heather providing flowering colour and at different points of the year and will require minimal maintenance. The use of heather in the roof makes reference to the Scottish building tradition of heather thatched roofs or "Heather Thekkit".

The Heather roof would be visible from the surrounding buildings and all four sides but also through the introduction of a Heather Wall acting as a screening device for the west end of the building in the form of a repeated window box. Now used as a wall surface, the flowering heathers will offer a seasonally changing façade to both user and passerby.

Heather Roof and Walls

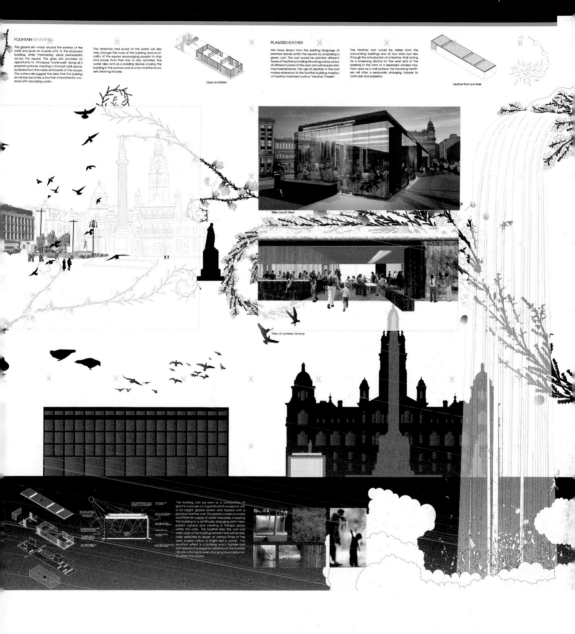

View South West

View of covered terrace

'he building can be seen as a culmination of granite outcrops on a granite plinth wrapped with a full height glazed screen and topped with a planted heather roof. The grassed screen provides a surface for a series of water cascades, wrapping the building in a continually changing semi transparent surface and creating a tranquil square within the cafe. The heather lines the roof and west walls of the buildings exterior and will be specifically selected to flower at various times of the year, purple, yellow or bright red in winter. The resultant effect is a building who's façade and roof reflects the seasons variations of the Scottish climate offering an ever-changing visual demand ity within the square.

Supplementary text

The information contained within the presentation drawings can be supplemented by accompanying text. This text is another important element in the design of a graphic presentation, and its display needs to be carefully considered; for example, it might be boxed out or weaved into the actual drawings. Remember, however, that this text is supplementary; the drawings should remain the primary means of communication.

As with the choice of line weight for drawings, the style and size of the font will affect the viewer's interpretation of the supplementary text. The hierarchy of the text and how this relates to the drawings should be carefully considered.

The rules

A graphic presentation is usually a complex mix of different levels of information, composed of several drawings that are displayed on the same sheet. It is therefore vital to adhere to certain guidelines in order to ensure that all the levels of information and different elements of content are read correctly.

All graphic presentations need a title. This may be the name of the building, or the title of the project, but either way it should appear in a larger text size so it can be read from a distance. Each individual drawing needs to be labelled clearly so that the viewer can immediately distinguish the plans, sections and elevations.

The scale of each drawing should also be clear. If several scales are used on one image then it should be easy for the viewer to distinguish which images use which scale.

As the drawings become more detailed the size of any text within them will become progressively smaller. To ensure that the information can still be viewed correctly, detailed drawings should use a numerical key or a legend, or incorporate symbols that allow the viewer to identify the different spaces or functions within the scheme.

Project: Metazoo
Location: Conceptual
Architect: CJ Lim / Studio 8
Date: 2000

This conceptual scheme explores an idea using photomontage; the architectural concept has been applied to an aerial site photograph. The idea is further explored in three-dimension as a series of the scheme's components are deconstructed to describe the idea in more detail. A legend associates each of the elements to the composite drawing.

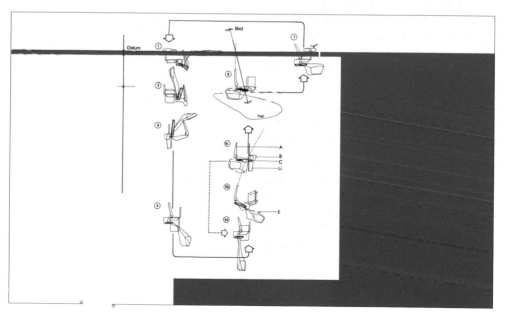

Avian membrane

A Avian membrane
B Tidal generator
C Clear acrylic end-plate
D Retractable rubber barrier
E Synthetic fluid membrane
F Pump/ Oil store/ Lighting deck
G Oil dispersion buoy
H Spectator seating
I Refuel/ maintenance socket

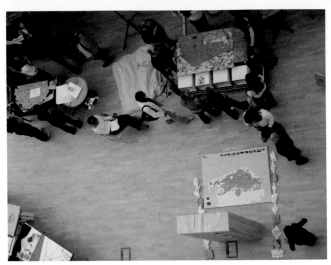

Graphic presentations are often accompanied by an oral presentation, which is usually carried out by the architect or originator of the work. The oral presentation provides yet another opportunity to elaborate the concept underlying the scheme, explain the connections between the presentation images and describe the idea of the scheme in further detail.

When presenting a scheme orally, connecting the commentary to each of the drawings is key. A good oral presentation (like a good graphic presentation) tells the story of the design process, from initial concept through to the development of the scheme's details. Key aspects of the concept should be outlined at the start of the presentation to identify the primary drivers in the scheme's development.

Presentation and exhibition

When presenting or exhibiting a proposed scheme the images will form part of a story. Often the architect or designer will orally describe the scheme, and this animates the images and brings together the different strands behind the concept. In doing so the designer can reveal aspects of the idea that may not be apparent in the drawings and emphasise the important conceptual drivers for the project. Also, importantly, questions about a design can be answered directly.

The rules

In schools of architecture the oral presentation is called the 'crit' (or critique) or the design review. Oral presentations in professional practice (to a client) are referred to as a 'pitch'. Whether presenting to a client, colleagues or examiners, it is vital to ensure that you know your audience and have addressed the parameters of the project brief for your scheme.

The oral presentation is an exercise in the promotion of your design and your opportunity to convince the audience that it is both exciting and viable. When explaining a scheme it helps to refer to all the drawings, sketches and models in your graphic presentation in order to fully describe how the building will be realised and how it might function. Doing so will convince your audience that you have explored all the design possibilities sensitively.

The oral presentation should be executed much like a piece of theatre; it should be rehearsed, all the props (your drawings and models) should be present and your audience should be engaged at all times.

To me, the drawn language is a very revealing language, one can see in a few lines whether a man is really an architect.
Eero Saarinen

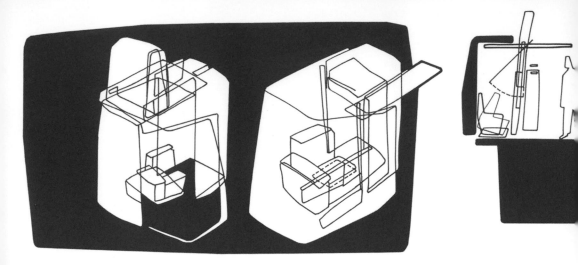

Project: Glass Stop Booth
Location: Conceptual
Architects: CJ Lim / Studio 8
Date: 2002

This sequence of images is explained in the form of a storyboard. The images are generated from a three-dimensional CAD model and each one shows a different view of the scheme and the structure both open and closed. Even though these are static, two-dimensional images they suggest the movement of the booth's panels to suggest how the user might interact with it over time.

Storyboarding is a technique often used by architects as a means to plan their concept or scheme. Much like a comic strip, storyboards are composed of frames that collectively explain how the architecture may be used or function over time. It applies a narrative to the design concept.

There are many ways for storyboards to be used as a successful presentation tool. They offer a means of describing and analysing the uses and functions of buildings or spaces over time, which means that the architect (or viewer) can critically appraise the scheme. Storyboards can also be used to describe a series of potential views of a journey through the scheme, which can suggest how the building may be experienced over time.

Storyboards can be constructed from freehand sketches, measured drawings or from a series of fly through images that are organised sequentially. Physical models can also be photographed and presented as a series of stills within a storyboard frame.

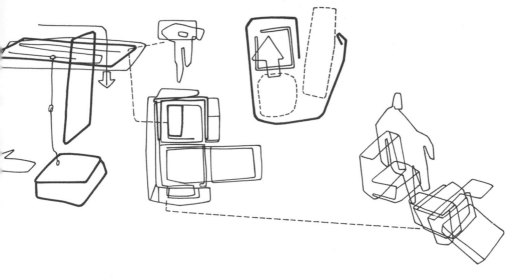

The storyboard can also be a very helpful tool in the design development process because it can represent spatial sequence, which means that the architect can visualise and consider connected or associated spaces. Additionally, storyboards can be used as a helpful means of planning graphic presentations or offering an overview of the connections and relationships between the different visual elements of a presentation.

The frame is a useful element of the storyboard as it separates the drawings and can allow different viewpoints of the same form to be presented.

Showing a proposed structure three-dimensionally allows the viewer to see 'around' the building form, which is particularly appropriate if the form is complex and multifaceted. Different views or aspects of a building form can be superimposed into a single presentation using framed boxes to highlight different elements of the scheme.

A portfolio contains representative samples of design work, and can be produced in both a physical or electronic format (or a mixture of media). Producing a portfolio is a design exercise in itself. It needs to communicate ideas and information clearly through a considered narrative, careful organisation and layout of information, and well-placed text and graphics.

The objectives of the portfolio

Like a graphic or oral presentation, understanding the needs of your portfolio's audience is the first step in its construction. Is it to be used to secure a job interview or a place on a course, or will it form part of a client pitch? The audience of your portfolio will affect both its content and its organisation. For example, a portfolio compiled to secure a place on an academic course will have to meet pre-defined criteria and demonstrate your competence and aptitude as a potential student. Similarly a portfolio that is produced for a job interview might display a range of work that echoes the style of your potential employer.

Defining the content, format and frame

Once the needs of the audience are established, the next step is to make a list of the drawings and images that need to be contained in the portfolio. A good portfolio will showcase a range of images, both freehand and computer generated, and from concept through to scheme details, to display different ideas across a range of media and representational techniques.

As with any presentation, the design of the images and their relationship to the format is key. It is useful to keep the format of all the portfolio's pages consistent. If this isn't possible then try to group pages together so the viewer doesn't have to keep turning themselves or the portfolio to view and understand the work.

living bridge   1887

Project: 'Living Bridge' portfolio
Location: Venice, Italy
Designer: Rob Moore
Date: 2006

A portfolio is a collection of work. This image, and those on the following pages, present a range or portfolio of images generated for a single architectural scheme in Venice called 'Living Bridge'

As well as the traditional drawings and sketches, images of a variety of different models have been included to show the extent of the design's process and development.

Physical portfolios may be framed in a wallet or ring binder (which can create a series of pages, much like a book), or a plastic wallet (although these can sometimes create a barrier between the drawing and the viewer and should be used carefully). If the portfolio is created on CD then the cover of the CD and the jewel case itself can also be designed.

Interactive web-based portfolios are becoming more and more commonplace. The content, format and frame of web portfolios is just as important as it is for physical ones. Online portfolios allow for a vast range of work to be displayed. Thumbnail images can be displayed on the site's home page and linked to their associated project images and information held elsewhere on the site, allowing the viewer to easily select and fully view the work of most interest to them.

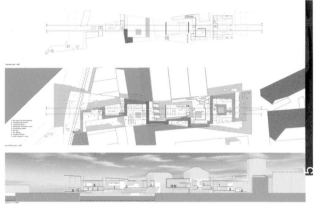

plans + section _____ 1887

Project: 'Living Bridge' portfolio
(continued)
Location: Venice, Italy
Designer: Rob Moore
Date: 2006

The drawings in a project portfolio, whether hard copy or electronic files, need to be carefully compiled and edited. Much like writing a story, the building design needs to be carefully described with a clear beginning, middle and end.

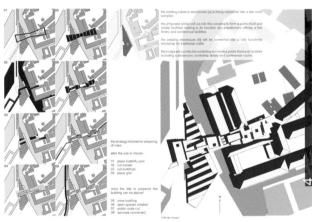

strategy _____ 1887

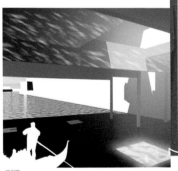

bridge _____ 1887

Integration

structure

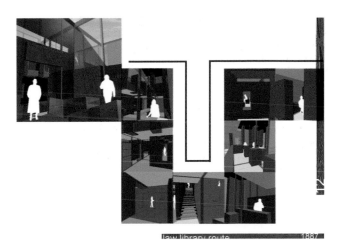

integration

law library route

law library model

Any portfolio, whether it is to be read online or as a physical set of drawings, needs to be carefully planned and edited, and doing so is a design exercise in itself. Ultimately the portfolio needs to address its audience successfully. In order to achieve this it is necessary to determine a brief for the portfolio and then decide on the range of projects to be shown in it. Making the portfolio interesting and engaging will help address your audience too. Organising the size and layout of your pages, as well as selecting a font style and size that is complementary to your work, are key considerations.

Title:

Sheet No:

Pages:

Constructing your portfolio

Planning a portfolio needs careful consideration and organisation, but using a storyboard framework can help you to organise the content of your portfolio.

Before you begin:

1 Determine the audience for your portfolio. What will they want to see?

2 Write an outline or brief for your portfolio.

3 Draw up a sequenced list of content (limit the number of pages or projects it will contain).

4 Consider the best format and layout of the pages.

5 Chose a font style and size that will complement your images. Remember you will need to use the font consistently throughout.

6 Consider the distinct sections of the portfolio (think of it like a book, there may be themes or projects that help to subdivide the portfolio's content).

Once these steps are complete you are ready to map out or 'flatplan' of your portfolio's pages:

7 Use boxes (much like those on the facing page) to denote the imaginary pages of your portfolio. Indicate in words and sketches the sequence of projects and the specific images associated with each.

8 Label each page according to the sequenced list of contents you compiled earlier (in step 3).

9 Consider how the pages connect to one another. Edit and revise as necessary until you are happy with the narrative.

10 Once you are happy with the narrative, assemble your portfolio so that is corresponds with the flatplan.

Flatplan

Using a flatplan to map out the contents of your portfolio will help enure that the projects on display are well organised, and that the pages address your intended audience in the way that you want them too.

Portfolios › Exercise 6: layout and presentation

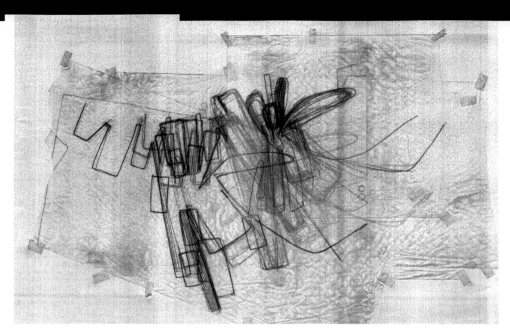

Successful representation of an architectural scheme or concept presents a challenge. To be a success, the form of representation needs to communicate the scheme's creative concept and its technical specifications.

Good architectural drawings and models require an understanding of the building's design. How this design is communicated to the audience via the architect's chosen media, form of representation and selection of layout and graphics allows architectural drawings to be ultimately variable.

Architectural drawings and models represent a future vision of a proposed building. Many of these proposals are never realised, yet architectural drawings possess a legitimate quality; the buildings they display could exist. As such they are not images of something that is, but something that could be and so need to have a persuasive power and to give confidence to their audience that the architecture could in fact be realised.

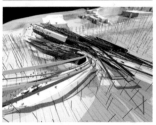

Project: Nam June Paik Museum
Location: Kyonggi, Korea
Architect: CJ Lim / Studio 8
Date: 2004

Architectural representation is heavily influenced by other cultural shifts in areas such as advertising, fashion and graphic design. The architect's drawing style must respond to these shifts; it needs to be culturally relevant and relate to the zeitgeist.

Plans and section drawings are specific devices that communicate architectural space and form, but beyond this, in the current climate of cross-disciplinary learning and teaching, architectural drawing has much to gain from its artistic neighbours in terms of rendering and representational techniques.

Architectural representation can be a straightforward practical interpretation of a proposal but, perhaps more importantly, it needs to inspire, to raise expectations and to transport the viewer into a world of imagination and possibility. An architect needs the eye of both an engineer and an artist to convince their audience of a new world of possibilities.

These CAD images are conceptual drawings that describe the architect's idea as a sketch in plan. Of the concept CJ Lim notes:

'The Nam June Paik Museum nestled within the pine forest... [the concept] evolved through a simultaneous proliferation of graphite lines, planes and ray-traced volumes. The butterfly wall is a visual metaphor for the white noise on an untuned television set, an unusual incidence of nature designed and constructed to mimic the electronic rather than the reverse.'

The images engage with the forms three-dimensionally and explore the lines and planes of the building as well as its relationship to the surrounding landscape. These engaging and exciting images are artworks in themselves. They describe a potential dynamic form engaged with a dramatic landscape.

Aerial perspective

A constructed view of a building or site from above, this kind of view allows an understanding of the context of the site.

Axonometric

Also known as planometric, this is a three-dimensional projection that uses a plan of a building space or object and rotates it through 45 degrees. The plan is then projected vertically to create a three-dimensional image. This is a quick and effective way to create a three-dimensional impression of a building.

CAD (computer aided design)

Computer-aided drafting or design systems are used by architects and students to develop and present their architectural ideas. The software can be applied in varying contexts. Two-dimensional plans are more effectively produced by some software packages. Others can create an impressive fly through series of images. Specialised software can render or colour images with realistic effects of materials, finishes and shadow.

Collage

This technique has been associated with painters such as Georges Braque and Pablo Picasso. It involves the assembly of fragments of images to create a new composite image.

Composition

When creating a presentation of architectural drawings, the composition of the images is important. A well composed image means that the information has been organised effectively so it can be easily understood.

Conceptual sketches

A concept is the driving idea behind any architecture. The concept starts at the initial design stage of a project and carries through the project as it develops

CPI (coordinated production information)

CPI is a system of communicating a range of scales for varying sets of information within architectural drawings.

Cutaway

A drawing technique that reveals an aspect of a building or interior space. The image has a section that is removed or 'cut away' to expose the inside of a building. It can also be used to explain how a building is assembled or constructed.

Detail

A detail drawing is focused on a specific aspect of a building. It needs to be drawn at a scale that allows aspects of material and fixing to be considered. This will normally be a full-size drawing or a drawing at the scale of 1:2 (half size) 1:5 (one-fifth size) or 1:10 (one-tenth size).

Dimension

Buildings can be measured as a way to accurately describe rooms and spaces. Dimensions are the measurement of these spaces. A dimensioned drawing will have recorded the size of rooms, walls, windows and doors.

Elevation

An elevation is the presentation of a face of an building or an interior wall. The elevation is designed through an understanding of the section and the plan.

Exploded drawing

An exploded drawing explains how a building is constructed or assembled. It deconstructs each element and component of the architecture and explains how they fit together.

Figure ground mapping

In architectural drawing the reference for figure ground comes form Giambatissa Nolli. During the seventeenth century he created a mapping description of Rome that depicted buildings as solid form and spaces as blank or empty areas. Figure ground maps provide a quick understanding of a city and its density. This is a technique now applied in a variety of contexts from urban analysis to spatial interpretation.

Fly through

CAD modelling has facilities that allow an architectural idea to be presented as a series of images to suggest a journey through a building or space. This series of images (or fly through) can be composed as an animated film as if the viewer is flying through the space.

Isometric

This is a three-dimensional projection that uses a plan of a building space or object and distorts it through 30 degrees. The plan is then projected vertically to create a three-dimensional image.

Juxtaposition

When placing drawings adjacent to one another there may be a sense of intentionally creating contrast of an idea or concept. Drawings of different scale can be juxtaposed in the same presentation.

Layer

CAD software uses the concept of layers to separate different types of information. These layers allow for changes to be made to different aspects of the design as it evolves. Each layer is a different drawing.

Layout

This refers to the positioning of images, drawings and text on a page. Layout is a critical consideration for the understanding of a scheme.

Legend

Drawings use codes and symbols as a form of shorthand. This shorthand is a legend, which not only displays all the symbols used in the drawings, but also explains their associated meanings. There are standard conventions and codes that are used to describe materials, fixtures and fittings.

Location plan

To initially understand a building or site proposal a location plan is needed. This will identify the site for the proposal and its immediate context. It will 'locate' the building and describe orientation and surrounding buildings and features.

Maquette

This is a small-scale model that represents and tests an architectural idea. A maquette can also be described as a sketch model or developmental model.

Object library

This refers to a library of elements available in CAD software programmes that are used in the creation of architectural drawings. There are many symbols for a variety of objects, from furniture to kitchen equipment, and these generic elements can be placed in a drawing to give a sense of scale and an understanding of function in a building or space.

Observational sketches

Rough sketches that describe what can be seen. Observational sketches are useful to record initial impressions of a site. These could record a journey, details or materials of the site. This process can reveal important issues for design consideration and inform the design idea.

Orientation

Orientation is one of the ways in which a building relates to its site. Orientation is described using the north point on the plan as a point of reference. Orientation refers to its relationship to the prevailing local climatic conditions such as the sun and wind.

Orthographic projection

This refers to the idea of representing three-dimensional forms as two-dimensional images. Orthographic projections usually take the form of plan, section and elevation drawings.

Parti

This is a type of drawing that reduces a concept of a building or scheme to its most simplified form so that it is easy to understand. Even the most complex building can be represented using a parti diagram. This is normally developed at the early stages of design and is a reference as the design evolves.

Perspective

This refers to the two-dimensional representation or description of a three-dimensional form or space.

Photomontage

This is a technique that merges one image of a building or object into another. CAD software allows for this type of image to be created quickly and effectively by merging digital photos or images.

Portfolio

A portfolio is a collection of information types. This can be comprised of drawings, photos, sketches or computer animations. A portfolio is usually directed towards a particular audience or a particular project.

Proportion

The satisfactory relationship of individual parts to the whole. In architectural terms, proportion can apply to the idea of a building design or to the idea of a presentation drawing. The overall presentation needs to be proportionally correct in terms of organisation and layout.

Render

A drawing can sometimes need additional colour or texture finish to describe materials or colour. When applying colour or texture to a drawing this is known as rendering.

Scale

When spaces are described accurately the drawings need to be to a specific scale. This may be metric (metres, centimetres, millimetres) or imperial (feet and inches) or some other understood system or module. Scale is described as a ratio. A full-size scale is 1:1, half size, 1:2 and so on. The appropriate scale needs to correspond to the appropriate level of thinking and consideration for the drawing, so a drawing of a street will usually be produced at 1:500 whereas a drawing of a piece of furniture is more usually produced at 1:5 scale.

Section

A section drawing is a vertical cut through of a building or space. This cut reveals connections within the building between different floor levels, such as double height spaces or changes of level. Section drawings can also connect to the outside.

Sectional perspective

This is a hybrid drawing combining a perspective drawing with a section drawing. This can suggest a relationship occurring inside the building and connect it with one outside the building. A sectional perspective turns a two-dimensional section into a three-dimensional perspective drawing

Storyboard

A storyboard is a visual framework that is used in many areas of design and graphic representation from advertising to film-making. It can be a useful mechanism that explains a concept as a series of images (a bit like a comic strip). Storyboards can suggest both time and visual description.

Superimposition

Images may be used collectively to describe an idea. Superimposed images are layered on top of one another to create a composite picture. For example, a sketch image superimposed on top or beneath a more formal line drawing of a plan or section.

Survey

A survey is a record or drawing that measures a space or building quantifying what exists.

Thumbnail sketch

A small sketch that describes an idea or concept in outline form. It is referred to as a thumbnail; due to its relative size it is effectively a reduced version of a larger image. Thumbnails are also used for referencing digital images or web images.

Visuals

Images of buildings that have been composed for presentation are sometimes referred to as 'visuals'. These may include perspective drawings, CAD drawings and photographs.

Worm's-eye view

This is a perspective view from beneath, as though viewing from underneath a building or space.

Glossary

The following books, websites, organisations and resources can be used as a platform for further exploring representational techniques in architecture.

Bibliography

Ambrose, G and **Harris, P**
Basics Design: Layout
AVA Publishing SA, 2006

Ambrose, G and **Harris, P**
The Visual Dictionary of Architecture
AVA Publishing SA, 2006

Ching, FDK
Architectural Graphics
John Wiley & Sons, 2003

Coop, D
Drawing and Perceiving: Real-world Drawing for Students of Architecture and Design
John Wiley & Sons, 2007

Dawson, S
Architects Working Details (Number 10)
Emap Construct, 2004

Doyle, ME
Color Drawing: Design Drawing Skills and Techniques for Architects, Landscape Architects and Interior Designers
John Wiley & Sons, 1999

Dubery, F and **Williats, J**
Perspective and Other Drawing Systems
Von Nostrand Reinhold, 1983

Gombrich, EH
Art and Illusion
Phaidon Press, 1987

Laseau, P
Freehand Sketching: An Introduction
W.W. Norton Ltd, 2004

Linton, H
Portfolio Design (Third Edition)
W.W. Norton Ltd, 2003

Lim, CJ and **Studio 8**
Sins and Other Spatial Narratives
Studio 8 Architects, 2000

Maranovic, I, Ruedi Ray, K and **Lokko, L**
The Portfolio: An Architecture Student's Handbook
Architectural Press, 2004

Mills, CB
Designing with models
John Wiley & Sons, 2005

Mitton, M
Interior Design Visual Presentation: A Guide to Graphics, Models, and Presentation Techniques
John Wiley & Sons, 2003

Porter, T and **Neale, J**
Architectural Supermodels: Physical Design and Simulation
Architectural Press, 2000

Reekie, RF
Reekie's Architectural Drawing
Architectural Press, 1995

Ruskin, J
The Elements of Drawing
The Herbert Press, 1987

Schank Smith, K
Architects' Drawings
Architectural Press, 2005

Styles, K
Working Drawings Handbook
Architectural Press, 2004

Materials and tools

4D Modelshop
The Arches
120 Leman Street
London
E1 8EU
Tel: +44 20 7264 1288
www.modelshop.co.uk

EMA Model Supplies Ltd
Unit 2
Shepperton Business Park
Govett Avenue
Shepperton
TW17 8BA
Tel: +44 1932 228228
www.ema-models.com

Squires Model and Craft Tools
100 London Road
Bognor Regis
West Sussex
PO21 1DD
Tel: +44 1243 842424
www.squirestools.com

Software

www.sketchup.com
Three-dimensional modelling software that can be used to quickly create basic models using plan information.

www.vectorworks.com
Relatively easy-to-use software, initially used as a two-dimensional drawing tool, which now also has three-dimensional facilities.

www.archicad.com
This software has very useful three-dimensional capabilities, and has a facility to create quick fly through images. Also has a rendering package to create impressive three-dimensional visuals.

www.googleearth.com
Software that connects to photographic maps of the world, which can be zoomed in and out to different scales.

www.photoshopsupport.com
Photoshop tutorials to give basic introduction to using Photoshop software.

Images

www.riba.pix.com
Part of the Royal Institute of British Architects, this site has a picture library with a search engine of a large range of architectural images.

www.gettyimages.com
Images can be downloaded from this site for use as graphics to complement architectural drawings.

www.archinet.co.uk
A resource-based website that provides good links to a range of other architecture resources.

Practice

www.architecture.com
A useful information site run by the RIBA that provides details about where to study in the UK and links to other practice and education sites.

www.eaae.be
EAAE is the European Architectural Association of Europe. Their site has information about where to study in Europe, and offers details about a range of courses and student competitions.

www.aia.org
The American Institute of Architects website provides advice and information on all aspects of American architectural education and practice.

www.uia-architectes.org
The International Union of Architects website has connections all over the world to professional and educational websites.

Contributors

6a architects
6a Orde Hall Street
London WC1N 3JW UK
Tel: +44 20 7242 5422
www.6a.co.uk

Alsop Architects
Parkgate Studio
41 Parkgate Road
London SW11 4NP UK
Tel: +4420 7978 78 78
www.alsoparchitects.com

Architecture Plb
St Thomas Street
Winchester SO23 9I ID UK
Tel: +44 1962 842200
www.architectureplb.com

Block architecture
83a Geffrye Street
London E2 8HX UK
Tel: +44 40 7729 9194
www.blockarchitecture.com

CJ Lim / Studio 8
Studio 8
95 Greencroft Gardens
London NW6 3PG UK
Tel: +44 20 7679 48 42
www.cjlim-studio8.com

David Mathias
Tel: 07852 260670
www.david-mathias.com

Design Engine Architects
3–4 St Clements Yard
Winchester
Hampshire SO 23 9DR UK
Tel: +44 1962 890111
www.designengine.co.uk

dRMM Architects
No 1
Centaur Street
London SE1 7EG UK
Tel: +44 20 7803 0777
www.drmm.co.uk

Dixon Jones Limited
6c The Courtyard
44 Gloucester Avenue
London NW1 8JD UK
Tel: +44 20 7483 8888
www.dixonjones.co.uk

Format Milton Architects
Format House
17–19 High Street Alton
Hampshire GU34 1AWUK
Tel: +44 1420 82131
www.formatmilton.co.uk

Hyde + Hyde Architects
8 Mill Field Sketty
Swansea SA2 8BD UK
Tel: +44 1792 420 838
www.hydearchitects.com

Jakob + MacFarlane
13–15 Rue des Petites Ecuries
75010 Paris France
Tel: +33 1 44 79 05 72
www.jakobmacfarlane.com

John Pardey Architects
Beck Farm studio
St Leonards Road
Lymington
Hampshire SO41 5SR UK
Tel: +44 1590 626465
www.johnpardeyarcchitects.com

Morphosis Architects
2041 Colorado Avenue
Santa Monica
CA 90404 USA
Tel: +001 310 453 2247
www.morphosis.net

Piercy Conner Architects
Studio A
Ground Floor, Jack's Place
6 Corbet Place
London E1 6NH UK
Tel: +44 20 7426 1280
www.piercyconner.co.uk

Pierre d'Avoine Architects
54–58 Tanner Street
London SE1 3PH UK
Tel: +44 20 7403 7220
www.davoine.net

S333 Architecture + Urbanism BV Ltd
Overtoom
197 1054 HT
Amsterdam
Netherlands
Tel: +31 (0)20 412 4194
www.s333.org

Steven Holl Architects
450 West 31st Street 11th Floor
New York NY 10001 USA
Tel: +001 212 629 7262
www.stevenholl.com

Witherford Watson Mann Architects
1 Coate Street
London E2 9AG UK
Tel: +44 20 7613 3113
www.wwmarchitects.co.uk

This book could not have been realised without the personal and professional support, encouragement, contributions and efforts received from a range of individuals.

Thanks are owed to the many architectural practices who have taken time to contribute their images and drawings to this book. A book about architectural representation can only be realised if architects are prepared to share their ideas and approaches to architectural drawing. Architects have traditionally learned through this altruistic approach to teaching and learning, and this spirit does still exist.

With this in mind I'd like to offer special thanks to:
George Wade at Alsop Architects
Graeme Williamson at Block architecture
CJ Lim at CJ Lim / Studio 8
Richard Jobson at Design Engine Architects
Russ Edwards at dRMM
Ed Jones at Dixon Jones
Matt Swanton at Format Milton
Kristian Hyde at Hyde + Hyde Architects
Dominique Jakob and Brendan MacFarlane
John Pardey at John Pardey Architects
Piercy Conner Architects
Dom Papa and Jo Woodruffe at S333 Architecture
Stephen Holl Architects
Witherford Watson Mann

Thanks are also due to The School of Architecture, University of Portsmouth 2007, specifically:
Professor Sir Colin Stansfield Smith
Paul Craven Bartle
Sian Crookes
Nicki Crowson
Jeremy Davies
Adam Hieke
Magda Kumala
Matt Mardell
Rocky Marchant
Rob Moore
Khalid Saleh
Edward Steed
Alex Wood
David Yeates and European Studio
(Martin, David, Jon, Jez, Gareth, Mark and Michelle)

Finally, special thanks to Simon Astridge who has helped with the organisation and picture research for the book, to Brian Morris, Caroline Walmsley and Lucy Bryan at AVA Publishing who supported the book throughout its evolution, and to Jane Harper for the book's wonderful design.

Representational techniques